6/17/18

Vickie,

Thank you for your support!
Speak love, joy, peace
and truth to yourself!
Be a Power-Thinker and
a Power-Taker!

Love

Dr. Mary Segars

Power Talk Begins with Power Thoughts!
by
Dr. Mary Segars, DSM

Dr. Segars can be contacted at:
Facebook.com/drmarysegars
Marysegars737@gmail.com
248-867-6092

Acknowledgements

I dedicate this book to my mother, the late Mary E. Johnson. She deposited so much wisdom in me and that was my real motivation to write this book. I want to thank God for my parents, who are both in heaven.

I thank my husband, Ezzell, who is my number-one cheerleader, and he's my friend and my love. Thanks for encouraging me to finish this book. Thanking my two beautiful daughters, Charmane and Theresa, for supporting me and loving me. Again, I have to thank God for giving me those two precious daughters and allowing me to be their mother. To my dearest grandchildren, Micah and Ernest. These two grandchildren have enlarged my heart so with love. Micah has developed into a fabulous young lady with so much wisdom, and Ernest is so wise beyond his age. I love my family so much.

I truly thank my editor, Gloria Palmer Walker, for her patience with a first-time author! She has been such a blessing to me.

Last, but really first, I thank my Lord and Savior for loving me and using me for His Glory!

Table of Contents

Table of Contents

Foreword

I want to thank you, the reader. I wrote this book because, for years, I spoke such negative thoughts to myself, and I didn't realize I was actually sabotaging myself. I had to learn how to *Power Talk* to myself, where I spoke about my strengths and my good attributes. What a difference that made in my life! So, my prayer is for you, the reader, to gleam from some of my strategies I've listed in my book, such as Affirmative Therapy. My ultimate goal is that this book will be beneficial to you, so you can speak powerfully to yourself and be the best you were created to be.

Enjoy!

Introduction

This book was birthed many years ago, but I believe the releasing of this book is timely, and it will fulfill two purposes. One purpose is to complete my doctoral degree from Destiny School of Ministry. After three years of studying and vast learning, the culmination was to write the dissertation. The second purpose is this paper will also serve as my book.

This book is about self-talk, which is what we say to ourselves, and the impact of our words. As outlined in the Bible, in the very beginning, God spoke and His words created everything. To have a powerful Power Talk that will motivate you, the reader, I will begin with what I call, 'Power Thoughts' and how we originate our thinking-patterns. Yes, many times, these thoughts we will discuss in the first segment stem from our childhood, our environment, and our surroundings. This can include your parents, caregivers, family members, friends, teachers, and church affiliations. What we perceive about ourselves can even be traced back to when we were in our mothers' wombs.

The Bible tells us in Proverbs 23:7a (NKJV): *For as he thinks in his heart, so is he.*[1] (*Note: All other Scriptures are NIV, unless otherwise stated.*) This is so true, as our thoughts are the barometer of what we perceive to be true for us. Our thoughts are developed in our early childhood through our parents, our environment, and our upbringing. Of course, those perceptions about ourselves can be changed by working on changing our mindset.

Thoughts are deeply rooted within us and we speak from our thought life. We think about things first, long before we actually act on those thoughts. I can recall when a minister explained about our thoughts this way: To better understand our thinking process, we must realize we can't control the thoughts flying around in our heads. They're like birds flying around in our heads. The birds represented different thoughts we might have, so different thoughts are flying around in our heads like birds flying around our heads. The thoughts can be good thoughts, or they can be evil or bad thoughts. See the picture of birds flying around a person's mind for a visual example of this concept (Picture 1).

Yes, it's true, Christians can have thoughts that are evil. The key is that Christians will not act on those thoughts because we have the power to cast those thoughts down through the pulling down of strongholds from our minds as stated in 2 Corinthians 10:4-5.[2] The weapons we fight with are not the weapons of the world. On the contrary, they have divine power to demolish strongholds. We demolish arguments and every pretension that set themselves up against the knowledge of God, and we take captive every thought to make it obedient to Christ.

To further explain our thought-patterns, the minister indicated we *can control* if the birds decide to nest themselves in our heads. In other words, we can reject it if those thoughts attempt to reside and nest in our head. Because once the thoughts are in our mind, we have allowed the thoughts or ideas to rest within our mind/head. Once a thought takes root in our mind, more than likely, we will proceed to follow through on those thoughts. See Picture 2 to clarify the nesting of birds in our minds.

Our thought-patterns are formulated in our childhood, and if a person has a negative thought life, of course, the person will generate a negative view of themselves. It doesn't just stop at a negative view of themselves, but extends to a negative view about life and other aspects of their life. I'm sure you know of people who always have something negative to say about everything. If you research why that person is so negative, it would reveal that person has a negative view of themselves because that is how they were wired from childhood and/or their environment.

Picture 1

Example: Birds flying around our head is a metaphor of thoughts flying around in our mind.

Picture 2

*As Christians, we have the power to not allow evil thoughts
to rest in our minds.
This is a metaphor of this principle, where we have allowed
the birds to take up residence
and live in our head. If we allow the thoughts to take root in
our minds,
it is more than likely we will act on those thoughts.*

"Great people talk about ideas.

Average people talk about things.

Small people talk about other people."

Author unknown.

"'They' Talked About Jesus Christ, So Expect 'Them' to Talk About You."

This was a real lesson my mother, Mary E. Johnson, taught me when I was in the third or fourth grade. My mother always told me, "They talked about Jesus Christ, so expect them to talk about you, too." At that young age, I just thought that was just something mothers say, because I really didn't understand the statement.

Since I was six years old, I've worn eyeglasses. As the sixth child and the baby of the family, I had a lot of nephews and nieces from my older siblings. I played with them as if they were my cousins. One time, I was playing tag with my nephews. We were running around the dining room table and my nephew Frank was 'it'. As he chased me, I quickly ran around the table and hit my left eye on the edge. As I hit my eye, Frank called out, "You're it." I started crying and my mother immediately applied pressured to my eye. Ever since then, I have worn glasses. I still have the mark on my eye. My mother always said, "Thank God, you didn't hit the corner of the table in your eye."

At that time, little girls had two choices of frames for glasses – either pink cat-eye-pointed glasses or blue cat-eye-pointed glasses. I picked the pink cat-eye glasses. I wore them to school, to church, and when I played. I wore those glasses everywhere, all the time.

In my fourth-grade classroom, a new student pointed at me and laughed about my pink glasses. I was so upset and I tried to ignore the new student teasing me. She had some of my friends join in on the teasing. They said I looked stupid with those pink glasses. I just wanted to get out of school and throw those glasses away. That day, I decided I was going to lose my glasses on purpose. As I walked home with my friends, I purposely took my glasses off and let them fall from my hands one block from my home. When I got home, I told my mother I'd lost my glasses. She was determined to help me retrace my path to find them.

Sternly she asked, "Did you leave them in the classroom?"

"No," I answered.

She took me by the hand and walked me back towards the school. One block from my home, she spotted my glasses on the sidewalk. I had hoped someone had stepped on my glasses and broken them, but no, they were waiting for my mother to pick them up. She instructed me to be very careful with my glasses.

"Keep your glasses on your nose where they belong!" she stated.

I didn't have the heart to tell my mother the kids were teasing me about the glasses and I'd purposely wanted them to be lost. My mother reminded me I needed those glasses to see the blackboard much better.

The next day in school, I prayed the new student wouldn't tease me today about my glasses. My prayer wasn't answered because the new student came up to me and told me how ugly I looked with those stupid glasses on, and she knocked them off my face. I was so angry that I hit the girl. The teacher yelled for us to stop fighting and that she was calling my mother. I had never been in trouble before in school, and I knew I didn't want my teacher to call my mother. I informed the teacher that the new student had knocked my glasses off my face and that was why I'd punched her.

The teacher told me to put my glasses back on and she sent the new student to the principal's office. All the other students were laughing at me because my glasses were crooked on my face. I took my glasses off and I really couldn't see the blackboard. I had to squint my eyes to see the lesson on the blackboard. That was the worst day of my life! I felt so humiliated.

After school, I stormed into my house because I was very upset.

"How was your day?" asked my mother.

I cried out, "Mom, they were talking about me today! The kids in my class called me four-eyed."

My mother stopped what she was doing and asked me, "What are you talking about, Mary?"

I yelled out, "They talked about me right in front of my face about my glasses. They kept teasing me and made fun of me!"

I was in tears and my mother knew I was crushed. She let me express myself before she spoke to me. She hugged me with so much love that day. She looked me in my eyes and assured me I'd be all right; then she said something I will always remember.

My mother began speaking softly. "Baby girl, 'they' talked about Jesus Christ and He was great, so you can expect 'them' to talk about you and me."

That was not what I wanted to hear from my mother at that time. I was hoping she would tell me she would come to the school and talk to the new student. I wished that new student would be put out of school for knocking my glasses off my face. I wanted revenge. My mother knew I didn't understand, so she shared a story to help me understand better. In her wisdom, she started to share the following with me.

"People tend to talk about people who are different from them. Also, often people talk about people who are doing great things. Jesus was great and He came to help people, but people rejected Him. They spoke bad things about Him which were untrue. Don't worry about what people say."

She further tried to console me. "You and I know that wearing glasses helps you to see clearly. You can see the blackboard to do your work. You have done an excellent job and that's why you are so smart. We are so proud of you and love you just as you are."

She was trying to make me feel better and it made me feel better for that moment. I knew my parents loved me. I had to acknowledged everything she told me were true.

After thinking about what my mother told me, it helped me to understand. I was reading at the age of three and I was writing at the age of four, so when I entered elementary school, my teachers recognized I was advanced, so the school double-promoted me. Being double-promoted allowed me to advance to the next level of school because I tested at a higher grade level. This double-promotion happened twice when I was in elementary school.

It really was years later when I fully comprehended the depth of what my mother had taught me. She had instilled in me self-confidence! That lesson helped me to take little stock in other people's perception of me, but to know my own self-worth. There was so much wisdom in what my mother gave me. My thought-pattern at an early age about myself has helped me throughout my life. It is so true that people will always have something to say about someone else, but the real measure is what I say about myself. I've learned we can't expect our spouses, our friends, our pastor, or our clergy to encourage us.

Just like David had to say unto himself, I have to encourage myself in the Lord. It is the same with us to speak to ourselves and allow God's word to infiltrate our minds and hearts. When we do this daily, out of our bellies, we will speak forth truth. We will speak with integrity and creativity. We are strengthened in our inner man because it is where we deposit God's word. So whenever we need to encourage ourselves, it will be available for us to dip into anytime we need it.

From my early teens, I've been aware that people will say things about another person without even knowing them. For a person's own self-thought life, a person needs to be assured about *who* they are as an individual, not rely on other people's opinions. As a Christian, my main concern is to make sure my life lines up with God's word. My mantra is: If I am pleasing God, then everyone else will have to align with it. As the Bible tells us: *Seek ye first the Kingdom of God and His righteousness . . .* Matt 6:33. (3)

We shouldn't have a problem with identity and self-image because, as believers, God spoke it out in Genesis 1:26: *"Let us make mankind in Our image, in Our likeness."* Certainly, I know my self-image is after my Heavenly Father and I have the DNA to prove it!

~~~~~~~~~~~~~~~~~~~

Ponder Thoughts:

Are you more concerned about what other people think about you or what God thinks of you?

_____

_____

_____

_____

What are your thoughts about yourself?   _____

_____

_____

_____

_____

_____

Our Thought-Patterns Regarding Relationships

Our thought-patterns have a critical impact on how we think about ourselves, about our relationships with others, and about our relationship with God. The purpose of God creating mankind is outlined in Genesis 1:26: Then God said, *"Let us make man in Our image, according to Our likeness; let them have dominion over the fish of the sea, over the birds of the air, and over the cattle, over all the earth and over every creeping thing that creeps on the earth."* Also in Genesis 2:18: *"It is not good that man should be alone; I will make him a helper comparable to him."* God was and still is very interested that mankind has relationship with Him and have a relationship with others.

According to Webster, the definition of thought-pattern is: a habit of thinking in a particular way, using particular assumptions. The Bible also has a definition of how we should think which is found in Philippians 4:8: *Finally, brothers and sisters, whatever is true, whatever is noble, whatever is right, whatever is pure, whatever is lovely, whatever is admirable – if anything is excellent or praiseworthy – think about such things.* This is not a suggestion or a recommendation, *it is a commandment from God!*

I'm not referring to positive thinking at all. I'm purporting that how a person thinks—whether it's about oneself or about relationships or about life—if the thinking process is based on the negative, then the results from thinking negatively will be negative. On the other hand, if a person thinks more in line with the truth of the Word of God, which is primarily positive, then the thinker will reap the rewards of positive thinking. For example, the Bible tells us all things are possible with God. (4) In the natural, a person will think, *'This will never happen in my life,'* and yet, if we begin to think according to the Word of God, and with God's intervention, that can happen in your life.

Joshua 1:8 is a key verse to tell us how to think. Furthermore, this verse goes beyond thinking for the reader, its instruction is to meditate, which is a deeper kind of thinking. Webster defines meditate: to engage in thought or contemplation, ponder, reflect; to consider as something to be done. That's the thought-pattern to have a powerful thought life, and that will transcend to a powerful talk.

Joshua 1:8: *Keep this Book of the Law always on your lips; meditate on It day and night, so that you may be careful to do everything written in It. Then you will be prosperous and successful.*

Many times, the difference between some people who rise above situations and excel in life and those people who will not rise, but will continuously struggle and never succeed in life, is really because of their thought-patterns. Before any action is pursued, there is a thought about that action.

The FBI interviewed a serial killer and determined this killer had thought about killing when he was very young and all through his teenaged years! He went through the entire scene of killing in his mind long before he actually performed the killings many years later. He described to the FBI that his mind was so focused on killing that to him it felt it had already happened.

Now on a positive thought-pattern view, I interviewed a very successful business woman who has her own public relations business. This woman was very confident and had a pleasant disposition about herself and others. She shared she started out as a clerk at a PR firm, but was always interested in how companies marketed their services and/or products. She searched out books and inquired of her colleagues. Many of her colleagues thought she should just stay in her area of expertise and let the professional be concerned about PR and marketing—in other words, stay in your 'clerk' lane. Of course, she went to school at night to complete her college degree. Those negative remarks did not discourage her, but gave her the determination to prove to herself she could fulfill her dreams.

She later explained, that because of her positive thoughts about doing what she knew she wanted to do, it gave her the leverage to go to school, pass the various exams, and excel in college. She also learned she couldn't share her dreams and goals with everyone, especially people who were against her. Some of her family members had a very negative outlook on life; she didn't share her goals and dreams with them. She often mentioned, if she had listened to the 'naysayers', she never would have accomplished what she knew she wanted to do. How powerful are our thoughts!

On a similar note about our thought-pattern, I was very good in school; however, math was not my strongest subject. All during undergraduate studies, I avoided taking math, but finally I couldn't delay taking it any longer because it was a required course. I'd told myself so often I detested math. My mindset was so firm about math because I had repeatedly told myself how much I hated math. If I said the word 'math', I would get a headache. It was so deeply rooted in my mind that my body responded, causing me to have a headache. That's when I fully knew and understood just how powerful our thoughts are.

After failing my first test in my math class, I immediately went to a tutor for assistance. My first encounter with the tutor wasn't a pleasant meeting. I mentioned to her before I even told her my name that I hated math. She looked at me and instructed me to stop telling myself that because, to pass this class, I would need my mind to be engaged in learning math. It took the entire semester for me to change my mindset about math, and with the help of a great tutor, I passed the math class—barely. Although I passed the math class, which was a required course, what I really learned was the impact of my thought-pattern. I began to think differently about math and had the pleasure of teaching math to my daughters, as well as my grandchildren. It all started with my thinking differently about math.

So let's discuss the thoughts a person has about themselves. I'm a strong supporter of how a person thinks about themselves is vital to how that person will think about others, about God, and about life in general.

Let's review the relationship God intends for man to have, because God is love and our relationship with God is based on love. As depicted on Diagram 1, it shows how the relationship with God can be. I refer to this relationship as a 'vertical' relationship. I use Romans 8:37-38 as a basic Scripture to show what's required to have a good and healthy relationship with God: *No, in all these things we are more than conquerors through Him who loved us. For I am convinced that neither death nor life, neither angels nor demons, neither the present nor the future, neither any powers, neither height nor depth, nor anything else in all creation, will be able to separate us from the love of God that is in Christ Jesus our Lord.*

In just living our lives, we realize things will happen to us, unexpected things, such as the sudden death of a loved one or losing our jobs. It could be so many things; nonetheless, it isn't so much what happens to us as it is how we respond or react to the situation or the issues. How we respond to any circumstance, good or bad, will be from our thought-patterns about life. Diagram 1 lists actions needed to keep our relationship with God solid, but before a person can actually do those things, our mind and our will should be in alignment to want to do those things.

According to Isaiah 1:19: *If you are willing and obedient, you will eat the good things of the land.* That statement is a conditional promise. Also, it's a two-part condition: First, you must be willing, and second, you must be obedient. God has given all mankind the power of 'free will.' Human beings have a choice: do what God wants us to do, do what the enemy wants us to do, or do only what we want to do. The choice is ours to make. However, Jesus proclaimed in the garden when praying to God the Father: "Not my will, but let your will be done." Jesus was willing and obedient, even until death. As Jesus displayed how to have an intimate and sincere relationship with God, so we must be willing and obedient to God. Christians, we must continue to strive to please God by keeping his Word. It is essential that we continuously practice God's Word.

Think about it: In a natural relationship, for example, a husband and wife have a covenant relationship. To have a vibrant and stimulating relationship with each other, it will require the couple to keep communicating with each other and loving each other. Many times, there will be misunderstandings or arguments, but that shouldn't end the relationship between the couple. No, not at all. There should be forgiveness and patience needs to be extended in every relationship. Relationships are very dynamic in nature because we're dealing with human nature. So it is with Christians to keep our relationship with God.

You see in Diagram 1A the actions and functions we need to keep our relationship with God in order. This requires our thinking about these items before we can actually perform them. These actions are done on a continuous basis, not just in a Sunday morning service. If you think about it, when you first received Jesus as your personal Savior, it was a decision you made after you thought He is what you need in your life—a Redeemer and Savior. I refer to this kind of relationship as a 'vertical' relationship because it involves you and God.

The next relationship I want to discuss is our thinking-patterns about ourselves. The Bible clearly tells us we should love our neighbors like we love ourselves. God has given us permission to love ourselves. We can acknowledge that God loved us because He gave His only begotten Son, who died that whosoever believed on Him would have everlasting life! So our love for ourselves is necessary for us so we can love others. [5]

Diagram 1

To make sure our relationship with God is vibrant and constant, we need to do the following:

Prayer	Study the Word	Live a holy life
Fellowship with God	Read the Word	Witness to others
Praise God	Attend church teaching God's Word	Speak in tongues
Communion with God	Fast	Dance unto God
Worship God	Meditate on God's Word	Love God
Obedient to God's Word	Utilize God-given gifts	Glorify God

Diagram 1A

GOD

Prayer

Study the Word

Live a holy life

Fellowship with God

Read the Word

Witness to others   Vertical Line

Praise & Worship

Attend church teaching
God's Word

Communion with God

Fasting

YOU

I'm convinced that more people are suffering from self-hatred. That's right: people have been so ingrained with negativity in their life and it is natural to continue that negativity into their own life—never satisfied with the way they look, how tall or short they are, and on and on. I'm sure a person would never admit they hate themselves, but their actions reveal it every day. When a person has no remorse about killing another human being, it could be directly related that they have no self-worth, so it's easy to kill another person. On the contrary, if a person can develop healthy and positive thinking about themselves, which might or might not have been enforced at childhood, then there could be a change in a person's attitude about themselves as well as about others.

I taught a seminar, *Abundant Life,* and one segment was about relationships. I instructed the group to be comfortable with themselves and to appreciate themselves. In other words, a person needs to be comfortable in their own skin. Love yourself because there will only be one of you *ever*. At our seminar session, we had an opportunity for the participants to speak this out loud to themselves and others: "I love me—the good, the bad, and the ugly."

We also discussed in the seminar that we are own worst critic. We, as human beings, are very critical of ourselves. Again, this could be because of upbringing or just being in a negative environment. Many times, we are the ones sabotaging ourselves by our negative thoughts, as well as the spoken words we use to describe ourselves.

The group had an assignment to go on a date with themselves at a place of their choosing, like to a movie or a nice restaurant. This exercise was given so one could learn how to enjoy their own company. They reported back the next week and it was quite amazing how many of the participants had a very hard time doing the assignment! There were some who accomplished the task, but explained they weren't comfortable with it. The assignment was given again and the results were somewhat better. It was shared with the participants that it starts with what you, and you alone, think about yourself.

I had a client who went through the one-on-one coaching session who was suffering from depression and basically didn't like herself very much. She had lost several jobs and had to return home; she lived with her mother. She thought her life was useless and worthless. This client met with me for one hour, and we developed strategies for her to begin to value herself and her skillset, abilities, and talents. She was encouraged to start liking herself, and ultimately, she would come to love herself.

We were making progress after several months of sessions, then something happened on her new job and she called me, panicky. She started speaking very negatively about herself and I stopped her. She realized she needed to stop that behavior or it would propel her into depression. After she calmed down, I gave her an assignment. I requested she make a list of the ten most positive qualities she possesses. This required her to stop and think. Initially, she didn't think she possessed any best qualities, but I reminded her that she was a very good listener and that's a great quality! She then begins to list her other qualities and went well beyond ten! At our next meeting session, she was in a very good mood and her image of herself was improving! It starts with how we think about ourselves.

The relationship depicted in Diagram 1B is the horizontal relationship which includes our family, friends, co-workers, neighbors, strangers, etc. It was explained that, if a person is having difficulty in the horizontal level of loving people, which is the low level of love, these could be the people who get on your last nerve, or someone who is very annoying to you, or perhaps someone who has given you a hard time. But, as Christians, we are commanded to love them. Yes, love the unlovable, as we are representing Christ. The problem is not with God, so the problem goes back to the person's thought-pattern. We think, if that person doesn't love me, then I don't have to love them either. It doesn't work that way.

When you are having difficulties in a low-level relationship, this could stem from your perspective because people might have hurt you through relationships. For example, if you find it hard to trust someone because you might have been taken advantage of in past experiences, you are preventing yourself from being hurt again. Because of past hurts, you will be very defensive as a self-protective mechanism, and you are walking around with guards around you to keep from being hurt. This type of self-protection we build into our lives can cause us to prevent people from having a relationship with us. To grow as a person, you will really have to allow the Holy Spirit to do a complete overhaul in your heart so you can begin to trust others and trust yourself about how you think about relationships.

Diagram 1B
Horizontal Relationships

Horizontal relationships include:

family members, friends, coworkers, neighbors,

in-laws, out-laws, people who tends to wrack your nerves,

etc.

It's interaction with other human beings.

Lower Level of Relationships

Since the lower level is where the problem is, the real problem is our relationship with God, which is the higher level of love. The Bible tells love covers a multitude of sins. All of us have formulated a mental image of ourselves based on the feelings of acceptance we received from our parents. Self-love emanates from God. Again, as stated in Genesis 1:26, we are created in the image of God!

Horizontal Relationships

I refer to relationships with people as horizontal. This is a lower-level relationship, in comparison to the vertical relationship between God and a person (see Diagram 1C). Often times, people, including Christians, will have problems at this level because it is having to deal and interact with other humans. True, this can be very challenging because some people are very difficult to deal with or to interact with. This list could include your family members, your church members, your coworkers, or neighbors. This could also include strangers, clients, in-laws, or perhaps your out-laws.

If we are having difficulties at this level in relationships with people, it is suggested we double-check our relationship with God. The Bible extols us to love our enemies and to pray for them. At this horizontal level, we could love the 'unlovable' people, the homeless and other indigents in the world. As we extend love to others, it will show the love of God to the dying world.

As you can see in Diagram 1C, the vertical line, which is the relationship between you and God, is much longer and more in depth. This is the kind of relationship God desires for his people to have with Him, which is very intimate and everlasting. It isn't an 'on-and-off' type of relationship. As the Word declares, He wants us to taste and see His goodness in our lives, and that requires a healthy and long relationship. God wants us to experience His new mercies every day!

Diagram 1C
Total Relationships – Vertical and Horizontal

GOD

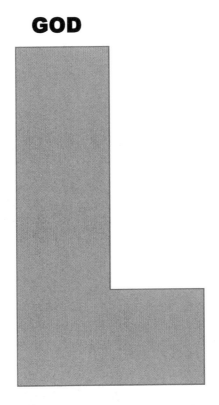

You   **Others**

Horizontal relationships are plural and those are our relationships with others. As Jesus explained, the first commandment is to love the Lord God with all your heart, mind, and soul. The second commandment is like it: We are to love our neighbors like we love ourselves. That's ongoing, but it requires the first commandment.

Also, notice these relationships (vertical and horizontal) resemble the letter 'L', which can stand for love. God is love. If we have the love of God reigning in our hearts, as well as have the Holy Spirit guiding us, and we are yielding to the Holy Spirit and God's word, we can love yet even our enemies.

As we developing an ongoing, healthy vertical relationship with God, truly that is a lifetime relationship. God is faithful, and as we continue in God's Word, we will learn to trust and depend on Him. It is recorded in the Word of God that He is the author and finisher of our faith. Then we can learn to develop good, healthy horizontal relationships with others; as shown here on this diagram, it forms an L. Let the L represent love and it begins with our thought-pattern.

Notice the vertical relationship is singular between you and God. A person cannot have a relationship with God along with their mother, father, or spouse. It is a personal relationship. It is between you and God only. However, the horizontal involves many relationships. First, the vertical must be stable and constant. It will facilitate the horizontal relationships to be more genuine. Also, it might be worth mentioning that the horizontal relationships may not always be ongoing. I say that because some people are in our lives, or we are to be a relationship with some people, for only a season.

For example, during my college days, I developed many friends and we had great relationships. After graduating, everyone continued on with their lives, and those relationships were different. We slowly separated, then we only occasionally reconnected. It just isn't the same type of relationship now. I realized that during school, we had so much in common and could relate to each other, but once we graduated, our season was completed. There was one dear friend and we are still very close in our relationship even after graduation. Even though we don't talk every day, we still maintain our relationship; however, it's different, but it is real. I like to think horizontal relationships are needed to really help us to hone our interaction and social skills.

Changing Our Mindset and Our Thoughts About God

How a person perceives themselves starts with a thought. Have you ever seen a beautiful and stunning lady, yet she thinks of herself as ugly? Yes, because her thoughts of herself are based on negative thinking. She might have been told in her childhood she wasn't 'pretty', or she might have had an experience in life when someone hurt her very badly, which could have wounded her spirit. The 'pretty' lady might have developed self-pity and felt she wasn't good enough or pretty enough, so she fed herself that thought to the point she believed it. That's why the thoughts we have about ourselves need to be the same according to the Word of God. We have the assurance that God knows us best—in fact, better than we know ourselves. The Bible lets us know who we are to God:

- We are more than conquerors.
- We can do all things through Christ, Who strengthen us.
- Greater is He that is in us, than he that is in the world.
- We praise Him because we are fearfully and wonderfully made; His works are wonderful.
- He will never leave us nor forsake us.
- Being confident of this, that He who began a good work in us will carry it on to completion until the day of Christ Jesus.
- Therefore, if anyone is in Christ, the new creation has come: the old has gone, the new is here.
- Therefore, with minds that are alert and fully sober, we set our hope on the grace to be brought to us when Jesus Christ is revealed at His coming.
- No weapon formed against us shall prosper.

- He has come that we might have life, and life more abundantly.

According to Josh McDowell, we actually rob ourselves when we don't think we are who God says we are. An inadequate self-image robs us of the energy and power to properly relate to others.[6] If Christians can just receive and believe what the Word of God tells us about ourselves, we will develop a healthy self-image. McDowell described a healthy self-image as seeing yourself as God sees you—no more and no less.

We see the world and people through our self-image. Oftentimes, many people can't enjoy themselves because of the following reasons:[7]

1. Pessimistic outlook on life.
2. Lack of confidence in social skills.
3. Extreme consciousness about appearance, performance, or status.
4. Fear of being alone.
5. Defensiveness in behavior and conversations.
6. Inability to accept praise.
7. A critical and judgmental view of others.
8. Use of anger as a defense to keep from getting hurt.
9. Inability to express emotions.
10. A tendency to develop clinging relationships.
11. Fear of intimacy, because it might lead to rejection or a smothering relationship.
12. Self-defeating habits and behavior.

This is just a partial list, but in Appendix D, there is a list with additional reasons people could have a poor self-image. We might attest that we've witnessed some, or all, of these behaviors in ourselves or perhaps someone we know. In fact, I have a friend I've known since childhood. I'll call this person Gwendolyn, and she exemplified many of these characteristics. Gwen grew up in a dysfunctional family. She lived with her mother, her stepfather, and one sibling. She never felt love from her mother. All during her school years, this young lady was a loner and never had any real friends. She was a below-average student, and she'd lost any interest in achieving academic standards. It was almost like she was invisible. She thought no one cared for her. What was happening behind closed doors in her home made her feel ashamed and unworthy.

She experienced years of feeling unloved, disrespected, and useless. She never understood why her mother never believed her when she informed her that her stepfather had attempted several times to have sexual intercourse with her. Her mother eventually threw her out of their home and she lived with other relatives. Again, Gwen felt abandoned and unloved. Of course, this low self-esteem image of herself carried over into her adulthood. According to her, she was just existing. This person never felt real love, and she was involved in many bad relationships with friends and with the opposite sex.

She eventually was introduced to Jesus as she attended a church where the Word of God was taught. She learned so much about a loving God and so much about herself. She was very skeptical about the Christians in the church, even though they shared their faith with her and showed her love. After years of not trusting people, Gwen continued with her defensive behavior, even though she was saved. After continuously going to church and Bible study, Gwen slowly began to trust God, Whom she could not see. She later explained that trusting God because of the Word of God was better for her because she couldn't physically see God. If she was going to be disappointed again, she couldn't see Him and it wouldn't be so hard to handle. However, as she continued to read the Word of God, she realized that God loves her so much and she learned to love herself as the Word of God states for us to love ourselves. Of course, this didn't happen overnight, but she was steadfast in learning to trust God, His Word, and eventually, to love others.

There are so many Christians like Gwen who are struggling to accept themselves and the person God made them to be. There should be classes for newly-converted Christians to fully understand who they are in Christ. Future church leaders will need to know their sheep, and it can be very challenging not to assume that all Christians are at the same level and in the same place. It isn't being realistic to think that because clearly the Bible tells us the wheat and the tares should grow together, and when it's time, the chaffing will happen.

One resolution to help a Christian become the person God destined them to be before the foundation of the world is to have a comprehensive study about who they are as a Christian now that they are in Christ Jesus. This kind of teaching would strengthen a new convert's faith to fully understand what Jesus did by dying for them, and the new convert would know they are forgiven.[8] Once they know all their sins are forgiven before God according to the Bible—God will not condemn them for the bad things they have done, good things they have left undone, and any wrong things they have thought about—what a freeing experience! Also, they will know they are reconciled with God.[9] Because the new convert has accepted Jesus, they have reunited with God. Prior to accepting Jesus, there was a void in the convert's life. The anger that was between them is gone. They are no longer an enemy against God. It is Jesus Who has allowed us free access to God.

Another benefit of being a Christian is the new convert has been rescued.[10] It is a blessing to know we have been rescued from a life-threatening situation. Jesus paid the ransom for our lives with His own life. Sin no longer holds our lives hostage. Satan is not our ruler any longer once we're in the family of God! A Christian has been redeemed![11] And our lives are no longer a worthless debt to sin. We have had our life debt covered and our future holds an inheritance from God. We can look forward to rich meaning and purpose in God's future plan for us.

How good it is to know we are known by God![12]. We have been known and cared about all along, and God has been watching out for us from the beginning. God has cared and loved me from day one. It is a blessing to learn that I was chosen, [13] I have been handpicked by God, and my salvation was not accidental. God intended it for me. If, as a new Christian, we can grasp that God is intentional and He was there all along, we will be more willing to come to Him without shame. We were blinded and didn't acknowledge Him . . . God called the Christian out for salvation even though we do not deserve it. We deserved what Jesus received—death—yet, Jesus was our substitute so we could be reunited with God. What an awesome sacrifice by Jesus.

Once a new Christian develops their faith more in the Lord, it could be realized that a new convert has been justified before God.[14] When God hears our prayers, God has declared us innocent because of Christ. Jesus won our case by paying the penalty for us. We have been acquitted of all our crimes. That's such refreshing news to Christians. This needs to be taught so new converts will learn to mature in the things of God. This will transform their minds, and Christians will have a new mindset and thinking process by learning these principles.

Someone like Gwen, who's never felt accepted, only rejected by loved ones, can find acceptance in God.[15] We have been welcomed by God and are no longer rejected. Christians are no longer on the outside, but are in the inner circle of God. In other words, Christians are in God. So many new babes in Christ have asked, "What am I saved from?"[16] That's a fair question because the new convert will not feel any different on the outside or will they look any different, so what is salvation really all about? The child of God will know God has rescued us from God's just anger/wrath. Saved or rescued from sin. Rescued from death.

Christians will be rescued from themselves because in our society in the United States, people are prone to live their lives the way they want to and do whatever they want to do. Frank Sinatra put it this way: "I'll do it my way." Once we are in God, we learn to do it God's way! The Bible tells us the thief comes to kill, steal, and destroy, but in God we are saved from death, as we will live forever more in Him. Last, but not least, we are rescued from Satan and a sinful system.

Another benefit for a Christian is the assurance they have been chosen.[17] To fully understand that God, Almighty God, personally handpicked His people. Our salvation was not accidental; God intended it for you. It's so refreshing to know God called each one of us out for salvation, even though we don't deserve it.

More than not, many Christians experienced harsh and cruel events in their lives before accepting Jesus as their Savior, Redeemer, and Deliverer. Once they allow God to minister to them personally, it is so comforting to know in God we are now justified.[18] God has declared us innocent because of Christ. When He looks at us, God sees the precious blood of Jesus, and then we are justified. Jesus has won our case by paying our penalty for us. We have been acquitted of all our crimes. Jesus is better than any lawyer because He paid the ultimate price. He gave His life for all who will receive Him.

As a Christian, it is very rewarding to appreciate and recognize we are accepted by God.[19] Others might not accept us or understand us, but our God has accepted us, just as we are. He will develop each of us into the person we should be and people can't do anything about it. The reward a Christian can cherish is that God has welcomed us. We are no longer rejected. We are no longer outsiders. We have the best when we have God. That's real security in God, and true assurance that God's acceptance is so much greater than a human being's acceptance. It's knowing that God bought us with a price and we belong to Him.[20]

Have you ever been in a situation where you went to the grocery store to purchase food for your family? You entered the checkout line, the cashier rang up your food items, and the amount of the food is displayed on the cash register. You look at that amount with outstretched eyes because it is more than the money you have? Oh, yes, I've been there before. The cashier was waiting for me to pay for the items, and I was asking the cashier to take this item off. Now I don't want this or I don't want that. It's embarrassing and the people in the line behind you are rolling their eyes at you for holding up the line. What do you do? You can't pay for your everything, so you put some things back.

However, with God, as a Christian, we have been paid for—in full—by God. God owns us. In reality, we no longer belong to ourselves. Our old way of life no longer owns us. This happens automatically on the inside of a Christian; however, with teaching and being obedient to the Word of God, our lives will be transformed from the inside out. Our old behaviors will be replaced with God's Word. Living a life for Christ is a lifestyle, and our friends and family will sense that we are different and there is a change in our life. It's because we are alive in Christ.[21] We receive new life from God when we become a Christian. For a Christian, our spirit has been brought to life and will never die again. Because of the fall with Adam, all mankind enters the world with the sin nature. When a person receives the call from God to accept Jesus and the person accepts the call, then and only then, will their spirit be quickened back to God. It makes our life here on the earth a blessing; however, there's so much more than what this world can offer. A Christian's body will be made new after we die and we will live forever. More importantly, a Christian will have a new meaning and purpose, and a new way of looking at life!

Once I had the opportunity to deliver a message that 'Freedom isn't free!' In essence, what Jesus did on the cross is for everyone who believes on Him, and it cost Him his life. Once a person accepts Jesus and receives His freedom, the cost to the Christian is to change their own way to follow God's way. Christians, we have been set free! We are no longer a slave to sin.

With so many hurting people and people really needing true love, it is a blessing for a Christian to know for sure that God deeply loves them.[22] There's no guessing about God's love for us because He has given us His most precious gift— His Son, Jesus. As much as we say we love someone, are you willing to die for them? Seriously, God didn't hesitate to offer His only-begotten Son for our ransom! What great love is that?! One cannot really understand this kind of love that only God can give. This agape love is unconditional and it isn't comprehensible because, as humans, we are so use to pseudo-love, which is based on what can you do for me so I can love you. Human love is a very selfish and self-centered-focus kind of love. What a great assurance to know we are loved because God's Spirit of love is in our hearts. Thank You, Lord, for your everlasting love towards us!

My sister-in-law raised her grandchildren. One had medical challenges and couldn't function as a normal child, so she was very concerned about his well-being if something was to happen to her. However, God assures His people we are taken care of.[23] God will let His people know we are secure in His hands. His word guarantees He will never leave us nor forsake us. God will never abandon us and He will complete his work in us. The Bible tells us God will supply all we need. Philippians 4:19 (KJV) states: *But my God shall supply all your need according to his riches in glory by Christ Jesus.*

It is important to teach the new convert that the benefits of being a child of God are endless, and that as we grow into maturity, God will cultivate in us His characteristics to give Him glory. When our minds are renewed, the realization will be apparent that we our new creatures in Christ.[24] We will have a new makeover of our minds and spirits.

This is similar to a book I read by Dave Ramsey, *Total Money Makeover*.[25] It emphasized the importance of taking control of one's spending habits and actually identifying where your money will go. It's a very informative book that elevates one's mindset to think differently about money. It teaches a person the proper way to have a relationship with money. The same with a new person in Christ. It is a new way of thinking and allowing God to develop you. It's the inner self that has been recreated after a new model of human being— Jesus.

The greatest realization for new converts is that they are born of God and have entered into the family of God. They are now a children of God, after the likeness of Jesus. As the Bible tells us, Jesus is the 'firstborn' example from the dead of what we shall be in the resurrection. It's exhilarating to be welcomed into the family of God.[26]

The Jewish people were God's chosen people. God in His wisdom extended salvation to the Gentiles, and we have been adopted, or grafted in, as well. We are no longer orphans, and because of Him, we can share in the glory of being God's children. Furthermore, we are children of the promise.[27] We are children of Abraham, therefore, promised children! We are spiritual descendants of the father of faith. Our calling is to carry this Spiritual heritage into the world. We have an awesome work to do for the Lord. It is a pleasure to know we are friends of God as John 15:15 states: *"I no longer call you servants, because a servant does not know his master's business. Instead, I have called you friends, for everything that I learned from my Father I have made known to you."* Truth is, we are servants of Jesus Christ, yet He calls us friend.

Christians can be thankful to be citizens of heaven.(28) We are members of God's heavenly Kingdom and our true identity is with the people of God. It's true because this world is not our home.

As Christians grow into the things of God, we are blessed with every Spiritual blessing. Let's not fret about what those in the world have because we have been given unfathomable riches in Christ, and that's just the tip of the iceberg of the countless blessings He has for us. God will unfold to His people their purpose, and we are His workmanship. It is so important to recognize we are a temple for the Holy Spirit! The very fact of knowing we have God living on the inside of us. That's why the Bible tells us to "be Holy, for I am Holy."(29) This is important for new and mature Christians as we value the fact that this is serious business with God. We are to represent Him and be different than the world. The Holy Spirit is such a gentleman and will not go against our free-will. He wants us to be obedient because we want to do what is pleasing to the Lord. We always have a choice to do what's right. Again, it starts with our thinking process.

That's why, when I witness to new converts, I let them know their life for Christ may cause some friends to leave and they will acquire new friends. This is because we are a member of Christ's Body. Think of it as we are a part of a living organism bigger than ourselves. We all need one another to survive. If a Christian is suffering with something, then the body of Christ should intercede and comfort that one because we're all part of the Body.

The Bible instructs Christians to meditate on God's word, and when we do, we can embrace the fact that we have God's seal of ownership[30] and have been made clean through Christ's life and death. Let our minds dwell on our purification and allow the Holy Spirit on the inside of us to reveal that truth to us so it is real in our minds, in our hearts, and in our spirits.

I share with young girls and young women in the Alternative for Girls organization. Because so many of them have been hurt and lied to so many times, this causes the young women to be insecure. However, after developing a relationship with some of the young women, I let them know that in God we are secure![31] Many times we don't understand why bad things happen in our lives, but we can trust and believe God will work things out for our good in all circumstances. With His acceptance, we are free from all condemnation and we can't let anything separate us from our God.

Again, that's the vertical relationship with God mentioned earlier in this book. Along with insecurity comes a sense that you aren't safe, but with God, we can be safe because He has anointed us and the word confirms that He has not given us a spirit of fear, but of power, love, and a sound mind. It is a process, and as Christians, we learn how to depend on God daily to provide for us. Eventually, as we continue to read God's Word and we will come to understand God will protect us and we can have the victory! Victory is ours because Jesus Christ is victorious and we are in Him! We are unstoppable when we are in Him. Christians can declare we are winners in the end because God is for us.

Now I can appreciate when my mother and my grandmother would sing praises to God for the great things He had done in their lives. It's my turn now because I understand for myself, and I know just how great God is to me.

Have you attended a funeral lately? I've noticed a great difference when I've attended a funeral for a nonbeliever than when I attended a funeral for a believer. The main difference is this: For a nonbeliever, the people are sad and without any hope. However, for a believer, the people are rejoicing because they know their loved one knew the Lord as their Savior and they will live with God for eternity. Even if the body dies, they will live again and receive a new body in the resurrection. This kind of thinking helps those in Christ because the Word declares it and believers know it to be true.

This quote captivates the thought-pattern:

**The happiness of your life depends upon the quality
of your thoughts;
therefore, guard accordingly.
Marcus Aurelius**

The Bible also tells us the same thing in Philippians 4:7: *And the peace of God, which transcends all understanding, will guard your hearts and your minds in Christ Jesus.*

Our minds cannot tell the difference if a thought is positive or negative. Once we think something, our minds will attempt to make that thought come to pass in our lives. Another way to put this is our minds do not filter out if this is a good or bad thought. It just stores the thought and will attempt to make it happen in your life.

Our Thought-Process:
How We Think About Obtaining Knowledge

The next thought-pattern I would like to discuss is how we think about knowledge or how we learn things. Yes, again, this is a mindset regarding our thinking process. This again was a lesson I learned from my parents. I grew up in a Christian home, so my parents were stern about the things of God as well as academic learning.

My mother and father always encouraged me to get my education, although she didn't go beyond high school. She attended Miller School in Detroit, however, she had a PhD. in wisdom and knowledge of life. My father attended college and obtained his degree in mathematics. My mother was a stay-at-home mother, and she let her children know a person can learn from anyone. Her remark about how you can learn from a fool: If nothing else, you don't want to mimic your life after a fool's life. Her encouragement to read caused me to be an avid reader.

Once I had a writing assignment when I was in high school that I discussed with my mother. I shared with her that my teacher wanted me to read about and write a report on abortion. I explained I didn't want to read the book and didn't want to write a report because it was against my moral values as a Christian. Being a wise woman, she let me share my concerns and why I didn't want to do this assignment. She instructed me to read the book with the determination to learn something new about the subject. As a teenager, I thought I'd learned enough about the subject from my church and from my parents. I was adamant this book wasn't a good read for me. She challenged me to read it and take only the things that would strengthen the moral beliefs I hold valuable. The rest of the book that didn't represent my values, I could dismiss.

My mother wanted me to know I shouldn't limit my learning by the way I think. She wanted me to be a well-rounded individual, not a close-minded person with limited knowledge. With that specific purpose, I read the book and truly learned information about abortion I did not know. Because the very subject was about abortion, I didn't want to read the book; however, my mother proved to me I could learn from the very things or subject I *thought* I couldn't learn from. I received an A+ on that essay and very favorable remarks from my teacher about my convictions.

I've used this principle today of 'eat the meat', or gain the knowledge, and if there is something contrary to my viewpoint or beliefs, 'spit out the bones', which is to eliminate that part of knowledge not valuable to you. If there is some knowledge worth keeping, retain it for further growth. Throughout my college studies, I've been able to utilize this method for my learning. It was necessary because there were many subjects, ideas, etc., that were in opposition to my view or my position. By doing this, I've gained worthy, insightful information, and there was no problem discarding what I referred to as 'nonsense' information.

I must mention, to utilize this method effectively, there is a caveat about this principle. For this principle to work properly, you must be fully-convinced and persuaded in your viewpoint, your position, before reading opposing positions. The reason this is so important is, if you are not solid about your beliefs or your position, when you read an opposing view, you could become confused or you could start to doubt your beliefs. Be steadfast and firm in your stance; then you can go up against any opposition.

Just a year ago, my granddaughter was going away to the university and I shared with her that schools, especially colleges and universities that are not Christian-based, can be very liberal in their thinking and will teach things that are contrary to your Christian beliefs. Yes, I shared this principle with her and let her know you must be rooted and grounded in God's truth and have a mindset that these are the principles I will value and live by. Just like my mother told me, we can learn from anyone. Be open to learn new things and other interesting things, but be firm in your beliefs. She expressed that nothing can separate her from her convictions about God, yet she would learn and understand many things, and judge any opposing views by the Word of God. In fact, several months before she left for university, we both went to see the movie, *God's Not Dead*. Her insight for a young person really encouraged me because the Word of God will not return to Him void, but it will accomplish what It was sent to do. We trained her up in the things of God at home and at church. It is a lifestyle.

This thought-pattern also happened to Jesus. The Sadducees and Pharisees challenged Jesus on various laws. Jesus was ready for their inquiries and schemes because He had the mindset that God's Word is supreme, and He would fully explain the verity of God's Word to the doubters. We need to have the mind of Christ as we are told in the Bible. When we think according to the Word of God, we are in a better position to stand up against the opposing view.

Romans 12:1-2 states: *Therefore, I urge you, brothers and sisters, in view of God's mercy, to offer your bodies as a living sacrifice, holy and pleasing to God—this is your true and proper worship. Do not conform to the pattern of this world, but be transformed by the renewing of your mind. Then you will be able to test and approve what God's will is— His good, pleasing, and perfect will.*

Let me discuss the thought-pattern that was instilled in me from my parents. In this 'Thought' segment, I will share some personal experiences that will highlight this concept that, "What a man thinks of himself, it is so."

The power of the tongue is so efficacious and that's why it is imperative we speak positive words to ourselves. I think about what Henry Ford once said: "Whether you think you can or think you can't, you're right." It goes back to our thinking. Power Talk begins with our thoughts. When we think positive about ourselves—our strengths, our potential, our skills, our talents, our life, and our environment—it will motivate us to speak positive things to ourselves. On the contrary, if we think about our weaknesses, our mistakes, and our failures, it will become a part of the fabric of how we perceive ourselves.

When I read and speak that quote, I am allowing my mindset to recognize that mistakes and failures are part of life; however, I will learn for the next time what not to do so I can win again. It isn't necessary to hold on to all the negative things that can and will happen to us. More important is, how we will respond to it? Rehearse it over and over again in our minds? There is no need for a pity-party, or to continuously talk about the negative thing that has happened to you. At that point, you are honoring the negative position, and the mind will try to manifest it again in your life as you continue to make it a part of your life. Move on and get busy with the necessary things in life to make you win.

We are programmed or brainwashed at an early age to think negatively. For example, if you can remember, as a child, we were instructed by our parents or our caregivers with "don't do this", or "you can't do that". As I think about it, what my parents were trying to instill in their children was simply to protect us from harm. I did it to my children because that was how I was raised. Even though they were trying to protect us, it was an incentive to do just what they'd told us not to do! However, the negative point was so programmed into our thinking process, it really takes time to re-program our thinking to not always think the negative thing first.

Case in point: My husband is a realtor, and in the fall or winter season, it gets pretty dark early. I can remember this one time, he called to let me know he had some showings that night and he should be home by 8 p.m. Now, let me remind you, in Michigan in November, that's pretty dark. As I was preparing dinner, I looked up and noticed it was 8:30 p.m., and my husband wasn't home yet. Yes, of course, I prayed all was well and prayed in the spirit, but my mind started to think the negative thing: Perhaps he was in a car accident and can't call me from his cellphone. I immediately called his cell and it went directly to voicemail, which tried to solidify my negative thinking. I attempted a couple of times to dismiss that car accident thought out of my mind, and I started to speak the Word of God over the situation, that all was well and my husband would be home shortly. Although I spoke it,

I didn't have the full conviction of my words; in other words, my thoughts and my talk were incongruent!

At this point, it was 9 p.m. I called my daughter and told her something had happened to Dad, and we needed to drive out to the place he'd showed the homes to try to find him. When I thought irrationally, it didn't make sense, because I didn't even know in what area he was showing the homes. See how illogically I was thinking? I didn't know. I allowed my mind to take me to a 'frantic' place, and when I can't think straight, I can't function right. By 9:30 p.m. my husband arrived home. He was so excited because his client had made an offer on the property he'd showed them. It was a very good thing for him, but for me, I was drained of energy because I'd worked myself up thinking the worst. I was almost hysterical because my mind had gone to the negative side of thinking.

What I learned from that experience and many other negative thoughts that had me 'caught up' in despair is, that is not what God wants us to experience. The Word of God is so true, and the Holy Spirit allowed me to think back to the Biblical days when there were no cellphones, no landline phones. Nevertheless, the people had to trust and depend on God. It was never God's intention to let us get so panicky that we can't think straight. I am still learning to trust God totally!

Another example of how important it is to be around like-minded people: Scripture reminds us we shouldn't be unequally yoked together because the two will not have anything in common. In the natural realm, I can remember when I wanted to start an investment club. I did the research on how to start an investment club and all the criteria to have a successful club. Next, I invited my family to a meeting to explore if we they would be interested in a family investment club. After the meeting with questions and answers, the consensus of the family was they were not interested in establishing an investment club. Many expressed they didn't feel comfortable having their money invested for a period of one-to-five years. I was somewhat disappointed; then I remembered I needed like-minded people to have a successful investment club. Another attempt with people who had indicated they were interested in an investment club resulted in a meeting where there was an affirmative reception of the idea. Why the difference? Simply the second group had the same mindset regarding investing and making their money multiple. The club was very successful and we scrutinized all future members of the investment club as we wanted only the like-minded people to join.

I've noticed in recent years that people are conducting meetings entitled Masterminds, and it's similar to having sessions with other like-minded people. These are people who want to meet with other people who might be interested in expanding their business or starting a business. Again, this group would be a 'sounding board' to bounce off ideas and different concepts. It is considered a 'safe place', where they are relaxed and free to speak without harm to others in the group. This is another example of the like-minded principle, and the reason to congregate with and share ideas or business concepts.

I want to make a distinction here because I am not referring to group thinking. Group thinking as described in the Bible can be found in Genesis, when the people wanted to build a Tower of Babel to reach God. The people wanted to build a tower, not with the purpose to worship the Creator, but to exalt the creation, and God knew their hearts were filled with evil. God wanted to disperse the people, so He confounded their language and the people were not able to communicate with each other.[32]

There's a tendency to have group thinking in churches. Again, God doesn't want that and the Bible tells us to study to show ourselves approved unto God, a workman that needs not be ashamed, rightly dividing the Word of truth. An example of group thinking in a church was the tragedy that happened with Jim Jones and his followers. Jim Jones, with his charismatic personality, had his followers to stop reading the Word of God, and to listen to him only. That's an extreme example of group thinking. The majority of his followers thought he was telling them what was best for them. As they continued in that mind-altering thinking, Jim Jones, as well as his followers, agreed to drink the poisonous Kool-Aid and committed suicide. God wants a personal relationship with His people, and the Church is the collected people, with each person having a personal relationship with God.

In the secular environment, group thinking can be displayed in gangs, because the gang members have to think like the gang leader, and to prove themselves, newcomers have to show they have the same thought-patterns as the leader. More often than not, the gang leader will make the newcomer do something to prove their loyalty to the leader. This initiation could be to hold up a convenience store, and to make sure there's no evidence of the crime, the newcomer must kill the store employee. This is truly group thinking to the point of brainwashing a person's mind to alter their thinking. Another example would be Hitler.

Other examples of our thought-patterns will be discussed now. Through my coaching with clients, many have shared they became what they heard throughout their childhood. When asked to elaborate further, one client mentioned her mother would say, "You are just like your dad." Or, her mother would tell her, "I guess I shouldn't expect much from you because you're just like your no-good dad." The person held on to those words from her mother until her adulthood.

After she shared that hurtful experience, she understood her mother was trying to correct her or warn her from being like her father. My client acknowledged that her mother would tell her those mean words in anger or when she was frustrated, but nevertheless, it was very mean-spirited and affected her self-image. My client realized she could not build a good relationship with anyone until she felt good about herself. She explained, when she became a Christian and received God's forgiveness, it was fabulous; however, it didn't immediately change how she viewed herself. It really took years to accept herself and to see herself how God viewed her according to His Holy Word. During one of our coaching session, it was recommended that she should never compare herself to another human being. If you just need to compare yourself to someone, compare yourself to Jesus.

In the Word of God, Jesus came to show how a person can truly live a fulfilled life for God. Sure, we can expect to mess up, but we have an advocate, Jesus Christ, Who can put us back again in the right position with God if we ask for forgiveness. He will cleanse us from all unrighteousness if we ask Him. Our lives are not to be compared to another person's because God made each of us unique, with a different purpose. When we attempt to measure up to God's standards, then we know we have the victory. Human beings don't have a heaven or a hell to put anyone in, and in fact, no human could ever die for anyone's eternal salvation. Only Jesus.

I had an opportunity to participate in an Inner Healing and Deliverance session, and it was an eye-opening experience for me. I'm only sharing the outcomes of the sessions and how crushed this person felt because they felt they had been programmed for failure. Because of a poor self-image and viewing oneself as a failure, one person unconsciously would seize opportunities to tell people off, stomp out, and could not deal with the hard issues and questions. Although the person desperately wanted to be successful, they really knew their mind was programmed for failure.

When a person can process information in their thought life, this can be referred to as critical thinking. When you think critically, you're actually analyzing things thoroughly. In the Bible, it is mentioned in Isiah 1:18: *Come now, and let us reason together, saith the Lord; though your sins be as scarlet, they shall be as white as snow, though they be red like crimson, they shall be as wool.*

I just want to concentrate on the portion, *Come now, and let us reason together, saith the Lord.* To me, this is where God wants to give us time to really think, analyze, digest, and ponder how we think. We know He was warning Israel about what she had done before Him. However, God wants us to do critical thinking about ourselves, our lives, and our conduct—in fact, everything about our lives and what our lives would be without Him.

In the secular world, people are always doing some kind of critical-thinking to process the 'what-if' scenarios in our lives, on our jobs, or for our families. This is the beauty of how God gave every human being the capability to think. However, critical-thinking requires extensive and expansive thinking. Critical-thinking is necessary to solve problems.

As I was studying for my coaching certification, it was very exciting to learn about the various thinking techniques to allow people to do deep-diving-thinking, much more than surface-thinking. I refer to surface-thinking as the first thing that pops into our minds, and more often than not, we speak those thoughts right out. My mom, of course, had a name for this kind of thinking: "Open your mouth and insert your butt." It is really true. Have you ever said something you wish you could take back? I know I have, more times than I care to mention. For instance, I have a close friend and we have shared many things together, but I hadn't seen her in a while. The next time I saw her, she looked different to me. I went up to her, hugged her, and without thinking, I said to her, "Oh, I didn't know you were expecting. When is the baby due?"

She looked at me as if she wanted to slap me and replied, "I'm not expecting, and you didn't have to say that to me because I've picked up weight."

I felt so bad and apologized to her immediately, but it seems like our relationship hasn't quite been the same since I did the "open my big mouth and insert my butt" to her. I'm sure we've all been there before by doing something like that. That's true surface-thinking. I didn't give any consideration to the sensitivity of that statement I made to her nor the other people around us who heard me. Honestly, I wasn't trying to be malicious towards her, I simply did not think through before I spoke.

The following are examples of critical-thinking that really help a person to be better prepared when talking and performing in life.

- The Fishbone Diagram can also be called a cause-and-effect diagram. It is a visualization tool for categorizing the potential causes of a problem to identify its root causes.

- Mind-mapping is another tool that can expand our thinking. Utilizing this type of tool will allow people to do brainstorming. Many times a person can be very solo in their thinking or have tunnel-vision thinking. The former thinking process is primarily due to our upbringing and our safe mode of thinking. This is the way my parents did it, and I'll continue to do it and my children will do it as well. The Bible refers to this as traditions, and many times we won't even venture to other thinking because the traditions are so ingrained in us. Many times we don't challenge our own thinking.

This reminds me of a story I think you might find amusing. It was Christmas time and a mother was preparing her family a wonderful Christmas meal. She would have her family as well as her husband's family over, along with her children. One daughter, who assisted her mother in preparing and cooking the Christmas dinner, was in the kitchen very excited. The daughter handed her mother a pan to put the ham in the oven. The daughter, wide-eyed, watched her mother cut off one end of the ham, then cut off the other end of the ham, before she placed it in the pan. The daughter wanted to know exactly what to do when she had her family and she had to prepare Christmas dinner, so she inquired, "Why do we cut the ends off the ham?"

Her mother became a little frustrated with her daughter's questions because she knew there were so many other things she had to do to make this Christmas dinner special. However, she understood her daughter just wanted to continue this tradition of Christmas dinner for her family so she answered her daughter. "I really don't know, dear. My mother showed me this way and her mother showed her. It's just the way we do it."

Well, her daughter had an inquisitive mind and thought, *I'll just find out from Grandma. I'm sure she knows why.*

The daughter went to the living room and called her grandmother. When her grandmother answered the phone, she immediately inquired, "Why is it you and Mama cut the ends off the ham for Christmas dinner?"

The grandmother was startled because none of her daughters had ever asked her about the ham, but she was fascinated that her granddaughter wanted to know. The grandmother, almost embarrassed, told her granddaughter she didn't know why she did it, perhaps because her mother had taught her that way and that's the way we do it. The granddaughter wasn't satisfied with her grandmother's answer and thanked her anyway. The daughter called her great-grandmother and posed the same question to her. Her great-grandmother laughed and told her she was a smart little girl because she questioned the 'status quo'. The granddaughter insisted that her great-grandmother tell her the reason why it was a family tradition to cut the ends off the ham before baking it.

Her great-grandmother told her this: "Baby, I cut the ends off my ham because the ham was too big to fit into the pan; however, I don't know why they're cutting the ends of the ham off!"

The moral of this story is to be inquisitive enough to ask questions and find answers, and be willing to do research to satisfy that quench for knowledge. Too often, it's much easier to just accept rather than to actually roll up your sleeves and research something for yourself. When a person has conducted a thorough search for something for themselves, it is so much more appreciated, rather than when everything is always handed to a person. I think often of this saying: "When the student is ready to learn, the teacher will show up." Another one of my favorite quotes is by Jose F. Albers: "Good teaching is more a giving of right questions than a giving of right answers."

As it has been proven, the average human being only uses ten percent of their brain (mind), and when we stretch our thinking, it develops new thinking for a person. I have proof of enlarging my thinking capacity. I had just completed my undergraduate degree from Wayne State University in 1991, and I was really excited about continuing my education. Thinking back about it, my plan was to take the GMAT or the GRE to prepare for the master's program. A close friend who graduated with me with her undergraduate degree was planning to go to law school. She suggested we take a year off from school and travel. When she mentioned travel, my thinking about travel was when we traveled for family reunions, or my immediate family would go to Chicago, Toronto, or California. My thinking of travel was very narrow; yet, in my subconscious mind, I really wanted to travel the world.

My friend discovered one of the major airlines was offering a 'special deal' where we could travel to London, England, then to one other location in the world for $199 round trip. At first, I couldn't even image traveling overseas, but she was an experienced traveler, and she gave me the brochures and all the details about this special deal. I tell you my imagination exploded! I was able to allow my mind to open to all kinds of possibilities! I actually saw myself standing next to Big Ben in London, England, after studying the brochures. My mind went there before I actually visited. Of course, this was the first time I had to obtain a passport. I needed to make sure my husband would agree with this traveling adventure. I must say, my husband encouraged me to do it because he knew how hard I'd worked to graduate with excellent grades, along with working a full-time job. He knew my friend very well and thanked her for elevating my mind to think 'out of the box'. He offered that trip as a graduation gift and I really appreciated the gift.

Going to London, England, for ten days was one of the most exciting times of my life. Of course, I took pictures standing in front of Big Ben and the Bobbies. While we were there, we visited a 'pub' and ate fish and chips, British style! Because my friend had relatives living in London, we stayed with them and they really showed us the 'true' London. We also visited Edinburgh and other attractions that a typical tourist would not have experienced. It was a mind-blowing and adventurous time for me, and I made a declaration that my family and I would travel the world. We visited and shopped in Harrods, a luxury store in London, which was an unforgettable event. I still have my Harrods bag as a reminder!

The second trip we took through the 'special deal' was Sydney, Australia! Yes, I went 'down under'. We visited the Sydney Opera House! It was amazing, and really, I think that's why I volunteer at the Detroit Opera House, as I've learned to appreciate that kind of music.

What if I hadn't allowed my mind to even think that traveling to places I'd only read about in a book could be possible? My husband and I were the first in our families to go on a cruise to exotic places because we thought we could; we planned it out financially and made it happen. This is so true when the Bible tells us that the power in us (our minds) is more than we can imagine or think, and He can do exceeding and abundantly more than we can imagine or think. Thinking which develops our power thoughts will be congruent with our power talk.

Once I attended a seminar where the speaker was discussing being successful. However, my take-away from that seminar was the conversation about reflective-thinking. Within this segment, the presenter wanted us to reflect on ourselves. One of the open-ended questions was: Do you like who you've become? He wanted us to explore our thinking and challenged us: If we wanted to change, what would it take? He demonstrated it would take more than just speaking it: I want to lose weight; I want to lose weight. Okay, you spoke it, but you haven't lost any weight. It's more than thinking about you losing weight. It requires changes in our behavior, in our thinking, and in our actions.

My thinking is this concept is the 'half-full' or 'half-empty' glass metaphor. The fact remains, there is a glass with water in it, but it's the person's perception if it is half full, which stems from a more-positive viewpoint. Yet, there are others with the understanding that the glass is half-empty, and perhaps, it will be totally empty if I spill it or drink the half that's in the glass. Both viewpoints, according to their perception, are true for them. The latter position tends to lend toward being more pessimistic.

After attending a Millionaire Mind Seminar, we were taught that thoughts lead to feelings, which lead to actions, which lead to results. T. Harv Eker purports that wealth begins with thinking—having a new mindset. Some of the highlights of his book, *Secrets of the Millionaire Mind,* are: (33)

- Rich people believe 'they create their life',** while poor people believe 'life happens to me'.

- Rich people focus on opportunities, while poor people focus on obstacles.

- Rich people act in spite of fear, while poor people let fear stop them.

- Rich people constantly learn and grow, while poor people think they know enough.

**I want to point out that I don't totally agree with Mr. Eker that rich people believe they create their life. I'm a Christian and I know God is my Creator, and in Him I can do all things through Christ who will strengthen me. I understand conceptually he is referring to the person who wants to create wealth is not expecting someone other than themselves to create the wealth—it's not up to the government or any other entity to do it for that person— people with a mindset that I'm not expecting anyone from outside myself to make me happy, etc.

Up to this point, I have been making references to our thought life as well as what we say as all positive. I'm a realist and fully realize there's the opposing side, which is negative thinking and speaking all manner of evil. According to I Corinthians 15:33 (KJV): *Be not deceived: evil communications corrupt good manners.*

Throughout my research, I found many instances about the pitfalls of allowing your mind to think the 'unthinkable'. In our society, we hear almost daily about a serial killer or a serial rapist, and when those news stories are reported, it didn't just happen; those people had a mindset to do those hideous things and finally acted on their thoughts. We see TV shows entitled *How to Get Away with Murder* and millions watch that program! We can read about the first murder in the Bible when Cain killed his brother Abel, and God was not pleased about it.

The FBI analyzes many serial killers and often see a pattern. Many of the killers look 'normal' and actually behave normally—like maintaining a job, and interacting with co-workers and family members—just a regular person; however, the difference between a regular person and a serial killer is their thinking-pattern. It starts with a person's mindset, and if a person dwells long enough and hard enough about something demonic or evil, that thought can consume the person's mind, and I relate that to when the Bible talks about a reprobate mind. A mind that has no constraints and will act out those thoughts the mind thinks!

Romans 1:28 states: *Furthermore, just as they did not think it worthwhile to retain the knowledge of God, so God gave them over to a depraved mind, so that they do what ought not to be done.* The mind has been seared with such wrong thinking that it allowed the mind to deceive the person. The person will eventually act out what has occupied their time, thoughts, and feelings. Action will come forth. We don't even have to go to the extreme of killing; it's talking about a habitual habit. Research has shown that if a person is constantly doing something for a period of thirty-to-forty-five days, a habit will form, and it will almost be like second nature for the person to perform that habit. To that person's mind, it isn't a habit, but it's something this person does all the time. The mind is nothing to play around with. God wants us to use our minds by renewing our minds daily with His Word.

The core of all evil thinking is the devil. When the devil thought evil against the Highest God, Satan said in his heart, according to Isaiah 14:13-15: *I will ascend to the heavens; I will raise my throne above the stars of God; I will sit enthroned on the mount of assembly, on the utmost heights of Mount Zaphon. I will ascend above the tops of the clouds; I will make myself like the Most High.* Satan wanted to be God, but Almighty God would not allow that to happen. Satan was the second in charge, but with the evil thoughts generated within his heart, he wanted to be God.

Sometimes when a person is dissatisfied or discontented with their life or situation, there can be a tendency to compare themselves with others. If that kind of thinking is not controlled, it can cause people to think wrongly about the person to whom they are comparing themselves. If you want to compare yourself with someone, compare yourself against the Word of God. Am I striving to be all the Bible says I am? It's a daily mind exercise to fill our minds with the things that will help us to strive to be the best person we can be. In Appendix C, I have provided a list of words to eliminate from your vocabulary. Those words seem to automatically come out of our mouths because we are so prone to think negative or the worst-case scenario. Also, there is a list of quotes we can incorporate into our thinking and speaking. It's imperative we learn to integrate more good, healthy, and positive words into our lives by thinking a new way.

There are people in the world with wicked thoughts in their minds and hearts who have done much damage to our society. Take Adolph Hitler, for example. Under his leadership, he was responsible for the genocide of at least five million Jews and millions of other victims. His thinking was ruthless, and he was able to persuade others to follow and do what he wanted them to do for him. His demented mind was so corrupt, yet he thought what he was doing was right.

One more example would be Saul in the New Testament. He approved the stoning of Stephen, as recorded in the book of Acts. Stephen was a Christian and did not back down to the Sanhedrin, who hated God and the truth. While Stephen was being stoned, he looked up to heaven and saw the glory of God and Jesus standing at the right hand of God. Even while they were stoning him, Stephen prayed, "Lord Jesus, receive my spirit." Then he fell on his knees and cried out, "Lord, do not hold this sin against them." (Acts 7:54-60)

Here are some pointers to help someone stop thinking negatively:

1. Make a list of the things for which you are thankful. You should do this at least once a day. By making this a daily habit, it can help you focus on things to be appreciated and you will find many things to be thankful for.

2. Try to find something positive in every situation. It's so easy to find fault in anything and everything. It really takes a trained mind to find something good even in a bad situation. When we are going through difficult times, it isn't easy, but once we've gone through a crisis, it no doubt builds character in us.

3. Work hard on not complaining. Try to say something positive and see the good in people and situations. To accomplish this, you might want to take a fast (or a break) from watching the negative news daily.

    a. God's people murmured and complained, and even God wasn't pleased with the murmuring from his people.

    b. Whining is another component of complaining. If something doesn't go our way, whining won't fix the situation. Be willing to accept things you don't have control over.

A constant state of negativity can affect your quality of life. If that negative thought-pattern continues, a person can experience some of the following ills:

- Negativity can keep you from trying new things that could be something wonderful.

- It can keep you for maturing and learning how to cope with the challenges of life.

- Negativity can lead to sadness, depression, stress, and giving up on life.

- It has been proven medically that negativity can take away your energy and motivation. Instead of a go-getter, you become a hopeless case who cannot help yourself.

(See the list of words in Appendix C that are negative in nature. You are encouraged to eliminate these words and phrases from your life!)

It has always been my nature to be positive and speak positive. Now, of course, on occasion, I've gone over to the other side, but for the most part, I'm in my normal mode. Please let me tell you it isn't me, but the God in me Who helps me to focus. I give much credit to my upbringing, my mother and father's wisdom, my personal experience with God, and my willingness to do and say what is pleasing to God.

Colossians 4:6 drops in my spirit to remind me: *Let your conversation be always full of grace, seasoned with salt; so that you may know how to answer everyone.*

According to Mindset Habits[34], the mind consists of three parts: the conscious, the subconscious, and the unconscious. We'll briefly discuss each as outlined on Diagram 2 which depicts each section of the mind.

Diagram 2

The Human Mind

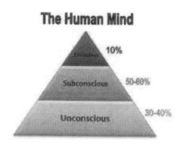

Science has proven the human mind can be divided into the conscious, subconscious, and unconscious, and they work together to create your reality. We can use the knowledge of how each functions to change a person's habits and create a happier, peaceful, and confident individual. Sigmund Freud was probably the first to popularize this concept into mainstream thinking. Freud created a useful model of the mind, which he separated into three sections—the conscious mind or ego, the preconscious, and the unconscious mind.

As the chart depicts, at the very top of the triangle of the human mind is the conscious mind. It has been claimed that humans only utilize ten percent of their brains. The next section is the subconscious mind, which accounts for fifty-to-sixty percent of the human brain's capabilities. In the last section, the unconscious mind is vast and deep and largely inaccessible to conscious thought. It could be thought of as the dark depths of an ocean. As displayed on the chart this section is thirty-to-forty percent of the human brain's capabilities.

For a better understanding of our minds, the conscious mind communicates to the outside world and the inner self through speech, pictures, writing, physical movement, and thought.

The subconscious mind, on the other hand, is in charge of our recent memories, and is in continuous contact with the resources of the unconscious mind.

Last, the unconscious mind is the storehouse of all memories and past experiences, both those that have been repressed through trauma, and those that have simply been consciously forgotten and are no longer of importance to us. It is from these memories and experiences that our beliefs, habits, and behaviors are formed.[34]

Think of our minds as computers. The conscious mind is like the keyboard and monitor. Data is input on the keyboard and the results are thrown up on the monitor screen. The subconscious mind is similar to the RAM (random-access memory) in the computer. RAM is where programs and data currently in use are kept so they can be reached quickly by the computer. It is much faster than other types of memory. Lastly, the unconscious is like the hard drive in your computer. It is the long-term storage place for all memories and programs that have been installed since birth. People who have been diagnosed with dementia do not have recent memories, but can recall memories when they were a child. The unconscious mind is being used.

The Bible stresses we have to renew our minds. Ephesians 4:23 tells us: *And be constantly renewed in the spirit of your mind [having a fresh mental and spiritual attitude].* (AMP).

Romans 12:2 tells us: *Do not conform to the pattern of this world, but be transformed by the renewing of your mind. Then you will be able to test and approve what God's will is—His good, pleasing, and perfect will. That is our humble service in the Body of Christ.*

Our 'mental apartment' could be referred to as the place where we keep our thoughts. Just like in a real life, we have things we keep around just because we want to. Oftentimes, those things might not be good for us or really have any value to us anymore, but nevertheless, we keep them around. Our mental apartment needs new furnishings, so perhaps we can replace the old furnishings such as negative talk about ourselves, negative talk about others, or maybe a negative outlook on life. The new mental apartment furnishings can be more good thoughts. Many times, we can be so lost in the big picture that we don't allow ourselves to dwell on the small and special stuff which can be good for our thought life.

For example, once I was sitting in my chair in my office at the real estate office, and it was the beginning of spring, which is the beginning of house hunting for clients. As I was sitting there, I thought I should call some of my past clients to inquire if they could recommend friends or family members who might be interested in selling or buying a home. I reflected that ninety percent of my real estate business was from referrals. If I pleased my present clients and did an excellent job for them, then maybe they would be kind enough to recommend me to people they know. But I didn't call any of my clients; I looked out the window and had a pity party all by myself.

As I was saying softly in my mind some negative things about my real estate business, a little bird landed on the branch of the tree right outside my office window. I stared at the little bird eating the fruit from the tree, and as I continued to watch the bird, the little bird began to chirp. The bird seemed so content with its life. Immediately, I took a picture of the bird and it didn't fly away. As I looked at the bird, the Word of God sprung up in my spirit to remind me that God is taking care of this little bird which does not toil or worry about anything. This tree will provide nourishment for the bird; how much more will your Heavenly Father take care of you. Wow! It was an 'aha' moment for me! I realized the bird had to fly over to this tree to eat. Also, the bird rejoiced because the tree fulfilled the bird's hunger. My mind was triggered sitting there and I enjoyed the silent moment as God spoke to me through this little bird.

My thinking was to email my clients or call my clients and get busy, because if I didn't make the effort to reach out, then I shouldn't expect something to happen in my real estate business. Just like the bird had to fly to the place to receive the food from the tree, it was necessary for me to make the connections with my clients. Needless to say, I got busy calling and emailing clients, and was able to obtain new clients by my efforts. I had to stop thinking the negative thoughts and think logically. If I wanted more clients, I had to make it happen by marketing myself.

Many years ago, I remember reading many books about how to be successful in sales, and the theme of all those books was the mindset of the salesperson. Most of those authors stressed, that if a person feels they are not in 'sales', to think differently, because a person is selling themselves to a prospective client or to a potential employer, etc.

When a person is confident of their abilities and talents (not arrogant), that is evidenced in that person's body language, and others perceive them as success. I like to think of it like this: It starts on the inside of a person (thinking) and it comes out for others to witness. This can be positive thinking or negative thinking, but it will be displayed on the outside.

God's Thoughts

The very thought that our Almighty God has thoughts! As recorded in the Word of God in Isaiah 55:9: *As the heavens are higher than the earth, so are My ways higher than your ways and My thoughts are higher than your thoughts.* Also in John 1:1-4: *In the beginning was the Word, and the Word was with God, and the Word was God. He was in the beginning with God. All things were made through Him, and without Him was not anything made that was made. In Him was life, and the life was the light of men.* The 'Word' in this passage is logos in Greek, which means 'thought'. That certainly confirms God thinks and developed thoughts, and we were created after His image and after His likeliness.

The Word of God's mission is to elevate our thinking so we can have the mind of Christ and to think on things above. This kind of thinking requires the believer to do this often, which requires daily doses of the Word of God. We have been told that faith comes by hearing and hearing the Word of God. The Word of God is powerful; the more we hear, study, and read the Word, it can pierce our old thinking patterns. Really, how can intelligent individuals comprehend and wrap their minds around the fact that a virgin had a baby? We can't even understand that phenomena! We just believe it because God said it was so. To have our thinking changed to conform our thought-patterns will take being thirsty and hungry for God's Word.

I recall when I first attended college courses and I wanted to excel in my classes, primarily because GM paid for my undergraduate and master's degrees. No, seriously, I wanted to do well for my own learning, but paid tuition was also a very good incentive. I studied so hard so I could fully understand the concepts and principles of the courses. It required that I read and re-read for comprehension, and I would quiz myself long before the actual exams. What I was doing was training my mind to concentrate, focus, and know the teaching material. I think back now, when the instructor would question the students, I would always be ready to answer because I'd studied and prepared to answer questions. Once, a fellow student in my class mentioned to me that I didn't have to answer all the instructor's questions. We became very good friends and we studied together. How much more will be required for believers to search, study, read, believe, and more importantly, do what the Word of God tells us. Again, I must repeat myself: The Word of God is not a recommendation or a suggestion; it is a commandment of God. For God to receive glory from our lives, we must submit to Him and be obedient to His Word. When we do this, with the help of the Holy Spirit, then and only then will we see growth in our lives.

When I was new in the Lord, my church at the time was adamant for new converts to become mature believers in the Lord. My Sunday school teacher, my Bible study teacher, and my pastor were on one accord to develop Christians. For one year, the focus was on John 15 and being connected to the Vine. Many church members stopped coming to church because it was reinforced week after week and month after month, but I was so eager to learn. The intent was to allow us to grow spiritually and to stay connected to the true Vine.

Let's look at this metaphor in the natural. I really appreciate plants. In my dining room in the corner, I have a beautiful aloe vera plant. When my grandson first gave me the plant as a gift, it was so small in a cute little pot. He decorated the pot with his own design. I called it 'Nesto's artwork'. He was so proud that he'd made the pot and his teacher had showed them how to plant the aloe vera plant in the soil. After a year, the little plant's roots began to grow on top of the soil and became crowded with 'pups' growing from the sides of the 'mother plant', and that little pot couldn't hold the growing plant. I decided to replant it into a bigger pot. The pot was much bigger to allow the roots to grow in the soil and the aloe vera plant grew upward as well. As the plant was growing, I used the stems of the plant for medicinal purposes. Once, I burned my finger while I was cooking, immediately went to the aloe vera plant, and cut a little from the stem to place on the burn. It was so soothing and I could feel it healing. After applying the aloe on my burn, there wasn't a scar or a mark at all on my finger. This plant served as a beautiful decorative plant in addition to having medicinal uses. Just as this plant needed to be planted in a larger pot to allow the roots to properly grow and sprout, which is a natural thing, similarly, for Christians to grow, we must stay connected to the Vine, God our Father. We need to think of ourselves as the Father sees us because we've accepted His plan of salvation by accepting His son, Jesus.

Jesus knew who He was and His purpose on the earth. He always let others know everything He said and everything He did was because His Father had instructed Him or told Him to do it. He was very obedient to His Father, even to the cross. Jesus came to show us how we can know our purpose, walk in our anointing, and live victoriously!

Another example of a person in the Bible changing their thought-pattern to identify with who God made him is Jabez. I am totally convinced Jabez had a different mindset and his thought-pattern was to expand his territory. According to I Chronicles 4:10: Jabez cried out to the God of Israel, *"Oh that You would bless me and enlarge my territory! Let Your hand be with me, and keep me from harm so that I will be free from pain."* And God granted his request. His mother named him Jabez, which in Hebrew means 'he makes sorrowful'. His mother stated, "I gave birth to him in pain." His name Jabez meant pain. The Bible mentioned that Jabez was more honorable than his brothers. I'm believing Jabez sought God and wanted to expand his thinking capabilities. We are not limited to mediocrity thinking—which is thinking like the world thinks. The world's thinking is there will always be doom and gloomy. Those thoughts are derived from their own experiences—things will just happen. There's 'no hope' thinking for the people of the world. Just look at the local or national news. The airwaves are filled with despair, and yet, they are reporting all this tragedy with a smile! Is this not absurd?

Let's talk about the fact that God is a thinker. His thoughts are supreme and true. When God thought about mankind, He had a plan for us. As stipulated in Psalms 139:1-18: *You have searched me, Lord, and you know me. You know when I sit and when I rise; you perceive my thoughts from afar. You discern my going out and my lying down; You are familiar with all my ways. Before a word is on my tongue, You, Lord, know it completely. You hem me in behind and before and You lay Your hand upon me. Such knowledge is too wonderful for me, too lofty for me to attain. Where can I go from Your Spirit? Where can I flee from Your presence?*

If I go up to the heavens, You are there; if I make my bed in the depths, You are there. If I rise on the wings of the dawn, if I settle on the far side of the sea, even there Your hand will guide me, Your right hand will hold me fast. If I say, surely the darkness will hide me and the light become night around me: even the darkness will not be dark to You; the night will shine like the day, for darkness is as light to You. For You created my inmost being; You knit me together in my mother's womb. I praise You because I am fearfully and wonderfully made; Your works are wonderful. I know that full well. My frame was not hidden from You when I was made in the secret place, when I was woven together in the depths of the earth. Your eyes saw my unformed body; all the days ordained for me were written in Your book before one of them came to be. How precious to me are Your thoughts, God! How vast is the sum of them! Were I to count them, they would outnumber the grains of sand—when I awake, I am still with You.

Wow, those are heavy-duty thoughts of God about us. If we can only believe God wants the best for us. Let's look at other thoughts our great and mighty God had. So many times, we ask our pastors, our teachers, and friends, "What do you think my purpose in life is?" Truly with all good intentions, they might try to give advice and counsel you about what *they think* is your purpose. I say that because I've had that experience—asking my parents, my spouse, and others what is my purpose—rather than going to the One who created me and asking what His thoughts are about my purpose.

As background information, I am the baby of six, as I mentioned earlier, and my parents were pretty much tired of parenting with five children in the family. However, I know my mother was more mature when she delivered me and had learned a lot about how to parent children. Being the baby, I believe I reaped the wisdom God had given my mother when I was born. Yes, I was unexpected, as my parents *thought* they were finished with adding to the family, but God *thought* differently. As I was growing up, I was always around older people, and God allowed me to absorb their wisdom and insight, which facilitated me being a mature thinker at an early age. Learning was very easy for me and my parents recognized that gift in me; however, they didn't understand how to nurture that gift.

I was probably seven or eight years old, and I always played school with my dolls and my friends. One summer, my friends and I were in my backyard on the porch, playing school. I was the teacher and my friends were the students. I welcomed them to class, read stories, and ask questions and they answered. We played practically all day. I would write short stories and poems to my students. I can remember my mother watching us from the kitchen window with a big smile on her face.

There was another time when we played in my backyard, and I was the preacher and my friends were in the congregation. Growing up in church, we tend to imitate what we see in the church. I had my little Bible and told them they must believe in God or they would go to a place they didn't want to go. I couldn't say 'hell' because I knew my mother would be listening and I didn't want to get into trouble, but I really meant that because I didn't want my friends going to that place.

One summer day, my mother mentioned she knew I should be a teacher because of my gift. I remember my dad agreed with her, but they both discouraged it because teachers didn't make much money, so they wanted me to go into business, not teaching. Their thoughts were for me to do what would make the most money and totally ignore the gift God had given me. Trying to please my parents, I went to college for business administration. After I got married, I mentioned to my husband I wanted to continue my education and pursue a master's degree. He thought I should continue in business administration with an emphasis in human resources administration. It was recommended because, "HR would complement you since you are a very loquacious person, and besides, you are a people person. Besides that, you really like people." I followed the counsel and advice from my loved ones—I knew they had good intentions for me to be my best—but what did God want for me?

Almost ready to graduate with my master's, many students and I had formed study groups to review and prepare for our exams. In every study group, the Lord would cause that teaching gift to rise up, and there I was teaching my classmates, ten-to-twelve students. Many shared with me they understood the teaching better than from our instructors and really appreciated the teaching. I felt encouraged by what my classmates told me and so I really sought God for His direction. I'll never forget, I was sitting out on my patio looking at the brilliant moon, and I started to praise God for how wonderful He was in my life and how even the stars and the moon glorified Him. In a moment of silence from me being in awe of the moon, I heard within me: "The moon has a purpose; how much more I have a purpose for you. How long will you waver between two opinions—the opinions of others and what I have called you to do?"(34)

I remembering crying to God and asking for forgiveness for not allowing Him to tell me what my purpose was—even before the foundation of this world! I was so filled up with His Spirit that I yielded and surrendered to Him, and wanted my thoughts to be what He wanted me to do in my life and through my life! I was changed by God that night and that was revolutionary. I know God freed me from seeking the thoughts of others concerning me and to always to look unto Him. I had a peace, that if I pleased God, everyone else would have to line up with what God demanded in my life. In other words, it is so much more important what God thinks of me than what man thinks of me. This is so liberating! For us to know what God thinks of us, we must know His Word.

I'll share another story about how important it is to think of yourself in a positive view because that will build up your self-image. My mother was an example of having a good self-image. She looked good for herself first, then for others. I can't recall a time when I didn't see my mom looking good at home. My mom would be up before I got up, then make sure I was all set for school with breakfast, etc. She had an infectious smile! I believe that's why I like to smile so much because of her smile. It's true, if you give a smile, you will probably receive a smile in return. That was my mom.

Even in her later years in life, she would smile with her lipstick on her lips. My mom liked to put on her red lipstick. That instilled in me to reach inside for my beauty! She looked good when my dad came home from work, and he really appreciated she wanted to look good for him. The truth is she was looking good for herself first, and he reaped the benefit of it as well. My mother really could have been a poet, seriously. Some of her sayings were comical, but nonetheless, those sayings were true. One of those sayings was, "You only have one chance for a first impression, so look your best and be your best. Only God will give us second and third chances."

Even today, I like to put on my flawless makeup that makes me look very natural, and of course, my lipstick must be on as well. It has been proven, when you look good, you feel good. Have you ever gone to a special event that was a 'black tie' affair? There is something about getting dressed up, and yes, that's on the outside, but it does something on the inside of a person as well. Isn't it so true? It has also been suggested that when you are sick or feeling bad, you want to stay in bed. It is better for you to get up, get dressed, and that alone will make you feel better.

After reading the book *The Millionaire Mind*, it intrigued me that millionaires are just like ordinary people, however, they think so much differently than the crowd.[35] The theme of the book indicated millionaires aren't any smarter or more intelligent than non-millionaires, but their mindset is focused on ways to take calculated risks, finding vocations that will afford them pleasure and fulfillment. Most millionaires write down their goals and keep their goals before them, emphasizing that visualization helps to stimulate their thinking. Our thoughts will turn into actions.

The Thoughts of God

God gave Jeremiah His thoughts towards him in Jeremiah 1:4-6: *The Word of the Lord came to me, saying, "Before I formed you in the womb I knew you, before you were born I set you apart; I appointed you as a prophet to the nations."*

God wanted Jeremiah to know with certainty what He thought of him. God is no respecter of persons. If we will allow Him to reveal to us our purpose, He will do it, but we have to want to know it from God and allow Him to work His plan in our lives. Just like Jeremiah, we often don't fully understand that our purpose is not for us, but for God's glory and for the world. What God wants us to do with our purpose is to give it to others so they might know God is alive and well and living big on the inside of us. We will display His glory when we walk in our purpose and in the anointing for our assignment.

In the secular environment, they refer to their purpose simply as, 'do what you love'. How much of the Christian world totally understands the concept that God has given us gifts, and according to the Word of God, our gifts will make room for us? Step out in faith and allow the thoughts of God to illuminate you to the point you will act according the Word of God, not by good intentions or our own interpretation of what God wants to do in our lives. My own favorite quote is: Your gift will lead you to your purpose. Mary Segars. [36]

Back to Jeremiah, when God spoke to him (apparently, it is implied God spoke to his mother also) in Jeremiah 1:5: *Before I formed you in the womb I knew you.* That's a deep thought from God. God knew what He wanted and His thoughts were, I know my plans for you and they are good.

God's thought toward Moses was He considered him to be His friend. Abraham believed God and God also called him friend. After the death of Moses, God's thoughts toward Joshua was to assure him that He would be with him and to encourage him. God's thought regarding Joshua were to let Joshua know he was a leader. God's thought about David was he was a king. David was the apple of His eye—a man after His own heart. Jesus, God's only begotten Son! God thoughts toward Him was He well-pleased with Jesus and He loved Him!

What are your thoughts toward yourself? Answer the following questions truthfully and find out if you, yourself, have good thoughts about yourself or evil thoughts about yourself.

▸ Question 1: Do you think of yourself as a person who enjoys life?

▸ Question 2: Are you often giving an explanation about your course of action or decision to others?

▸ Question 3: Do you seek the approval of others (boss, spouse, friends)?

▸ Question 4: Do you accept compliments graciously?

▸ Question 5: Do you have 'me' time with yourself? Schedule time just for you?

▸ Question 6: Do you encourage yourself (think about your strengths, talents, gifting, etc.)?

This little quiz is to jump-start your thinking about how you think about yourself. Of course, we don't think everything good or positive all the time, but there's no reason why we can't. I'm a realist and totally understand that our minds will respond to what we think, and as we'll discuss in the next segment, to what we say. I'm sure you've heard the saying: "You are what you think." As we understand more how our minds function, that is very true.

Let me elaborate more on this concept. As I was preparing to write this dissertation, every day the Lord would allow me to see or read additional information about our thoughts. One of my Facebook friends posted this post and I had to share it:

"There have been many wars and battles fought, but the greatest of these have been the war on the mind. It is so crucial to frame our thought life with God's Word to victoriously live this life."

That's exactly my sentiment! I also totally agree with the United Negro College Fund slogan: "A mind is a terrible thing to waste!"

When God created us in His image and His likeness, in His infinite wisdom, He created our minds with all its multiplicities, yet the Bible tells us to have the mind of Christ. If the Bible made a statement like that, it is possible to achieve it with the help of the Lord. We must submit to the Word of God and allow the Holy Spirit to assist us to be doers of the Word, and not just hearers only, or we are really deceiving ourselves only.

What are God thoughts toward you? Are you doing His will? Do you want God to say this about you: "This is my beloved daughter or my beloved son, with whom I am pleased." Those words were spoken to Jesus while He was on the earth from God the Father. According to Matthew 3:17, *And a voice from heaven said, "This is My Son, Whom I love; with Him I am well pleased."* We also can hear those words from God the Father, if we are doing what He has told us to do. Don't do it out of obligation, and don't do it with a 'bad' attitude. Do it because you want your life to please God!

Everything we do stems from our thinking processes. There was a quotation I saw that really capitalize this kind of thinking: "Fear happens in our life when we leave our minds empty." That just reiterates the importance stated in Proverbs 19:15: *Slothfulness casteth into a deep sleep; and an idle soul shall suffer hunger.*(KJV)

To survive in this world we live in, although we are not part of the world and its system, we must utilize our mind to think and always be diligent in seeking the truth of God's Word. When we mediate on God's Word, we will be able to exchange our way of thinking to the way God wants us to think and to do great exploits for Him.

Our Thought-Process Regarding Money

Again, thanks to my mom, she had a saying about my attitude and my mindset when it came to money. Her favorite saying when it came to money was: "When you're spending your money, you are the boss!" She stressed that point to me because she was a stay-at-home mom and she knew how to manage money. Money isn't supposed to rule you; you're to rule your money. My mom had to monitor household expenses, and she didn't play or pretend when it came to money. My aunt once mentioned to me, "Your mom could make a dollar stretch." My aunt would make gestures with her hands, expanding her hands outward to emphasize how much my mother could stretch a dollar. We would laugh about it, but it was so true.

How my mother instilled this principle in me was when I was ten or eleven years old during the Easter holiday. She wanted to take me to shop for a new dress for Easter. My mother didn't drive so we walked to the main street then we took a cab to the stores. My father's working didn't deter my mother from handling the business she needed to get done. Once my father suggested he would take her wherever she wanted to go on the weekend, but she didn't want to wait until then because all the good selection of clothes would be gone by then.

So, we were in the store and she decided on this beautiful dress for me, but it didn't have a sales tag on it. The saleslady was quite busy when we reached the counter, but my mother wanted to know if the dress was on sale. The saleslady didn't know, so my mother requested to speak to a manager who would know. When the manager came out, my mother was very polite and professional, inquiring if the dress was on sale. The manager checked and searched for a similar dress to compare the price. The manager found a dress, but it wasn't like my dress and he wanted to charge the same price. However, the manager didn't know my mother was a master negotiator. My mother informed him what she wanted to pay for this dress and he agreed. As we left the store to go home, my mother told me, "When you are spending your money—money that you worked hard to earned—you are the boss of your money." She continued with, "Don't let someone else tell you how to spend your money." I realized later in life that truth about money. Money is a tool to be used wisely.

Another example of how I came to understand that I must be responsible as a good steward with my money was when I read and reread the book written by Gail Perry Mason and Glinda Bridgforth entitled: *Girl, Make Your Money Grow*. The book really detailed how important it is to have the right mindset about money. It helped me think about money, debt, and how to handle these issues within my budget. There's no need to live paycheck to paycheck because we don't have the fundamental principles of how to handle our money. It really comes right down to our mindset about money. It challenged the reader to write down all your income, your expenses, and determine your net worth. From that point, start assigning your money to pay God, pay yourself, and pay off debt, with the understanding that debt-free is the ultimate goal.

During my quest to change my mindset about money, I would listen to Dave Ramsey on the radio, then I started to read his books about *Money Makeover*. It was a turning point because my mind was being renewed with strategies on how to leverage my life about money. The Bible reminds us in I Timothy 6:10: *For the love of money is a root of all kinds of evil.* Some people, eager for money, have wandered from the faith and pierced themselves with many griefs. We are to love God and seek His wisdom about being a good steward with the money we have. Everything we need is in the Word of God, as a reminder from the Lord.

Deuteronomy 8:18 states: *But remember the Lord your God, for it is He who gives you the ability to produce wealth, and so confirms His covenant, which He swore to your ancestors, as it is today.*

It is always good to be mindful that it is God who provided us with talents and gifts so we can accumulate wealth. It is so crucial to know and remember Him as our source for everything. As we are faithful to God in every aspect of our life, He will reward accordingly as Proverbs 28:20 promises: *A faithful person will be richly blessed, but one eager to get rich will not go unpunished.*

Again, my dear mom had a saying about everything, even about money issues. "If you obey God concerning your money, which includes reaping and harvesting, you really don't have to listen to others—especially when they are not giving you any money—about how to handle your money." My mother would say exactly what was on her mind and she didn't care who didn't like it! I think she really ingrained that same disposition in me as well. As long as I am pleasing my God, oh well . . . everything and everyone else will fall in line with God.

I attended a Millionaire Mind Experience and the session had some questions so the participant could glimpse what were their thoughts, feelings, and perception about money. Listed below are a few of the questions to answer and to analyze.[37]

The person should answer if they agree or disagree with the statement. The answer ranges from 1, meaning totally disagreement, to 10, total agreement. It's amazing the perception people have of money.

1.   Money is the root of all evil.

2.   It's more enlightened to be poor than rich.

3.   Having a lot of money will make me less spiritual or pure.

4.   Getting rich isn't for people like me.

5.   I'm too young or I'm too old to get rich.

6.   I'm just not 'meant' to be rich.

7.   Investments are for people who have a lot of money.

8.   It's not right for me to be rich while others have nothing.

9.   You can't strive for wealth and be happy and fulfilled at the same time.

10. I'm not educated enough to get rich.

Those are just a sampling of the kind of questions the participants addressed during the workshop session. Truly, I've learned more about how a person can cherish money, perhaps due to the lack of money during their childhood. I must reiterate that money is only a tool to be used by people.

Thought-Patterns Regarding Work Ethics

Let's continue to discuss our thought-pattern about other things as well. I'll go back to my childhood environment because that's where we all develop our character, our mindset, and attitudes about life, people, and ourselves. Even though my mother never worked outside her home, she was very cognizant of good work ethics. She displayed it in our home and she made sure my dad was always on time and ready to function at his best while he was on his job—the same way she taught me about being diligent and establishing good work habits.

It just might be safe to say my mom was *almost* a perfectionist because she knew what she wanted and she wanted it to be done right the first time. She keeps stressing that it takes more time and energy to do the same thing twice, so do it right the first time. When you do it right the first time, there won't be a need to repeat it. When it came to doing chores in the house, she insisted I do them right the first time. Being a teacher and a nurturer, she understood I am a visual person, so she would show me how she wanted something done right first. I knew my mother meant business when she was instructing me on how to do something. Take, for instance, wishing the dishes. This was a very valuable lesson for me because it took me once (maybe twice) to learn how to wash, dry, and put away the dishes in their correct places. We didn't have a dishwasher in our home; I was the dishwasher. (I will always have a dishwasher in my home.) When I was first introduced to washing the dishes, I thought, *Since I'm the baby, my mom will not let me do this chore.* Well, of course, I was wrong. She explained very carefully the importance of washing the glasses without breaking them. I couldn't let the dishes dry in the dish tray, but I had to dry and put them away in the cabinet. As I recall, it was one hot summer and I thought, if I quickly washed and put away the dishes, my mom would be pleased. Then I ran outside to play with my friends. Next thing I heard my mom calling for me to come back into the house. When I came back into the kitchen, my mom had removed ***all*** the dishes I had put up and wanted to know if I thought I had done a good job washing the dishes. She wasn't smiling, so I knew I had to be truthful with her. I nodded to let her know I thought I had done a good job. She handed me a plate I had put away and it had particles still on it. She made me wash all the dishes, dry them thoroughly, then put them in the cabinet, all while she stood there watching my every move.

Afterward, she shared with me, that if I had done it right the first time, I could have been outside playing, but see now it took much more time to redo what I should have done the first time. I truly learned how to wash, dry, and put away dishes the right way the first time. There was one other instance when my mom had me redo the dishes. I was sleeping, deep in my dreams, and my mom came into my room, woke me up from my sleep (how cruel is that!), and made me do it right. She was a keeper of her word.

Now let me make a declaration here. When my mom ingrained these principles in my mind, I didn't understand them at that time. In fact, I thought my mom was a sergeant and was deliberately making me upset. When we do some retrospection about our lives, some of those defining experiences will explain why we are who we are today. This principle is very relevant, not only for doing chores right the first time, but that first impressions only happen once—that first initial time. I've learned to make a good first impression because that is the first and only time to have that opportunity.

When I interviewed for a job, I understood that making a good impression meant doing it right the first time. Making a good first impression required being prepared to illustrate my best performance to that person, who had little or no knowledge about me. Thanks, Mom, for that principle because I don't like to redo things over and over; I like to do it right the first time. To accomplish this, I might have to do some preliminary work or preparations before it is time to do it. It will be right because of my pre-work diligence. It pays off in the long run, so do it right the first time.

When I think back, my mom was a genius. This principle about do it right the first time has been proven in the manufacturing arena as well. When I was employed at GM in the Global Human Resources Department, one aspect of my job for the Executive Leadership Program for our executives was to arrange for the executives to tour GM's manufacturing plant. During the tour, the plant superintendent confirmed to us it is very costly to GM when it is necessary to do re-work. It is much more cost-efficient when workers are trained properly and complete the work in the first attempt rather than in the re-work schedule. It just makes sense.

I want to continue with how we think about our attitude. Even now as I reflect on my childhood days, my mom was my 'shero' because what she deposited in me is something I never could have learned otherwise and for that I'm grateful. I believe God shielded me and allowed me to see and to know what would be helpful for me years later, and that was through my mother.

Anyway, my mom had this saying, "If you're mad, you'd better get glad." Now you know how you feel when you are mad. You don't want to hear a rhyme like that because, for that moment, you want to stay in this mood called 'mad'.

I use to think my mom stayed at home so much and just had time to come up with new rhymes, but really there were so much truth in her rhyming. As I think about it, she was a quick-thinker to come up with some of these sayings/rhymes. Just so you know, I don't do rhyming. Okay, back to my mom and her sayings. She stayed at home but she had a very positive attitude about life. She stressed that life is too short to be upset and mad all the time. Her favorite "let me tell you something" saying was, "It takes more energy to be mad and sad than to be happy and glad." That was so true for her life because she loved to smile and laugh. I guess after six children, a husband, and a household to maintain, she didn't have time to be mad. Seemed like my mom knew when I was mad about something. The ironic thing was when I was mad and wanted to sulk in my madness, I didn't want to hear my mom telling me to get over it. Let me sulk! Have you ever been there before?

It was a Saturday morning and my mom wanted me to get up early and complete my chores. I had a different plan that Saturday morning: to sleep in late, then get up later to do my chores. *After all*, I thought, *I get up very early all during the week going to school so I deserve a break today*. Well, my mom didn't feel the same way I did on that Saturday morning. She entered my room without knocking and started to open the curtains, letting the daylight shine right in my face. I was upset. She instructed me to rise up now and start doing my chores. I frowned and started to complain about her waking me up, mumbling something low under my breath about I'd do it later. She looked me in my eyes and asked, "Are you mad?" I thought, but never uttered the words to my mom: *You know I'm mad, so why ask a stupid question?* However, I replied sleepily, "Yes."

She smiled and told me, "Well, you'd better get glad." Why did she smile when I wanted to be mad and pout about it? I knew my mom well enough that when she smiled that way, it meant she was serious. It was better for me to do what she told me, then I could do what I wanted to do later. Her smile was used as a threat and to make me see the light— which was always her way. Of course, I got up immediately and completed my chores.

There was another incident when my mother was teaching me how to iron pillow cases. How absurd because we only sleep on the pillow cases and I thought they didn't need to be ironed! I simply inquired why it was necessary to iron the pillow cases. Again, my mom smiled and without blinking an eye said, "Because I told you so. That's why it's necessary for you to do it." Of course, I got mad, then I remembered I'd better get glad about it. However, I decided when I grew up, I would not iron my pillow cases and sheets!

Being the baby of the family, I wasn't as 'spoiled' as my siblings thought because my mom didn't play that favoritism stuff. Okay, sometimes she did allow me to get away with some things my sibling probably wouldn't have gotten away with. Oh well, that's the glory of being the baby—special treatment!

On a serious note, this principle is not to allow anger to overrule your thinking or your happiness. There are a million and one reasons to be 'mad', but what good does it do you when you are mad? When my disposition is in a more positive mood, I clearly see the importance of not allowing things that have little value to make me angry and there's no need to sweat about it. A Scripture that explains this concept is found in Matthew 6:34: *Therefore, do not worry about tomorrow for tomorrow will worry about itself. Each day has enough trouble of its own.*

Truly life is too short to be angry, which stems from being mad and sad. As a suggestion, when you are mad or upset, go visit a nursing home and just look at the people there. This could quickly snap you out of despair because those people would love to switch places with you in a heartbeat. The Bible let us know as humans, we will get angry, as Jesus got angry, but He didn't sin. So it is with us. We are capable of being angry, mad, or upset, but take it to the Lord in prayer. We have the power to not allow that feeling to cause us to sin.

Look at Jesus. He was angered, but He did not sin. He threw the people out of the temple and overthrew the tables in the temple. He declared that His Father's house would be a house of prayer. He didn't allow that anger to control him because the next verses talk about how he taught in the temple many days, letting them know He loved them and wanted to teach the right things of God.

Let's look at the fruit of the spirit that's found in Galatians 5:22: *But the fruit of the Spirit is love, joy, peace, forbearance, kindness, goodness, faithfulness, gentleness and self-control.* Only you can control you. You have the power to control your temperament, your attitude, your disposition.

I was reading and a quote caught my attention: "Nobody makes you angry; you decide to use anger as a response," by Brian Tracy.

What my mother said to me was for my good, but I decided to be angry or mad about it. We all have the power to control our behavior, and if our mindset is deliberate, to take the high road and to comply with God's Word. If we decide to do it God's way, and our minds are accustomed to obeying the Word of God, then, and only then, can we have the victory. Just like we shower and brush our teeth every day, we must also feed our spirit and our mind with God's Word. I like to put it this way: The more we do it, the more we will be able to do it. Practice makes better. It will become second nature to us when we make it a regular part of our lifestyle. That's why the Bible tells us to be slow to anger. Anger's wrath can be dangerous if it is not corrected and controlled.

Ralph Waldo Emerson puts it this way: "For every minute you are angry, you lose sixty seconds of happiness."

Utilize that energy to make yourself glad, happy, and fulfilled. It has been proven scientifically that it requires more muscles to frown. In fact, it takes forty-three muscles to make your face frown. On the other hand, it takes seventeen muscles to smile. We should smile more just because! Trying smiling right now. Go ahead and smile. Here's a simply test for you: When you are out and about, perhaps in the mall shopping, I want you to consciously look at a stranger and give them your best smile. The stranger will either smile back at you, might nod at you, or will look away from you. Don't allow the ones who don't acknowledge you to affect your mood. Keep smiling! A smile is universal! If you smiled at someone in Japan and you can't speak Japanese, that smile just said 'hi' in Japanese. Try smiling; I think you'll like it. Make it a habit to smile. Look in the mirror daily and speak your affirmations (we'll talk about Affirmative Therapy in the next section). Not only will your conscious and subconscious mind receive those affirmations, but they will produce smiles from you automatically. Your face will enjoy it also!

I'm convinced my mom enjoyed her life so much because she smiled from the inside out. Even when she made her transition to be with the Lord, she actually smiled into glory. When I saw my mom sleeping in the Lord, she actually had a smile on her face! She smiled a lot on this side of heaven, she smiled when she went to heaven, and I believe she's smiling now with Jesus!

Another thing about smiling: It is contagious. More than that, when you smile as you think about someone you love, it can bring to mind the good memories of your loved ones. For example, when I'm thinking about my mom, I have to laugh because of something she might have said or the funny faces she would make. Laughter is good for the soul. I think some of us just need a good old, 'hearty' laugh—you know those belly laughs that come from the depth of your being, the kind of laugh that can have you rolling, even crying.

As I was writing this book, when my mind would wander off, I would immediately think about something funny or read a good joke, and I would begin to laugh. When I did that, it recharged me to continue with my writing. I know that sounds crazy, but I know the Word of God tells us laughter, or a cheerful heart, is good medicine; but a crushed spirit dries up the bones.

I am like my mother in this sense: I have noticed how some people like to make a mountain out of a molehill! Why? It isn't that serious. I just can't figure out why a person would want to allow so much negative drama in their lives. It could be because that person wants attention and that's one way to seek attention from others. It has been reported that a person with a more-positive attitude during medical challenges is more likely to come through surgery or procedures more successfully than a patient with a more-negative attitude. It's all in our thinking capabilities.

It's true, environment can shape a person's thought-patterns. My husband's parents had ten children and he was the eighth child. Being surrounded by drugs and crimes in their backyard, many people, not all, will accept that same kind of living because of their mindset: the way they think about themselves, their environment, and their lives. However, if you have the right mindset, you will not submit to that lifestyle and will explore other options in life. My husband, for example, would be in the library reading and studying rather than hanging out in the streets with the neighborhood friends. My husband had a very strong mind to make decisions for his life, and he is a leader who has never followed after his environment. He witnessed many of his friends and family members using drugs, and some even died from drug overdoses because of their environment. Environment can have an impact on your thinking; however, you can determine your destiny.

Interviews Conducted for People's Thought-Patterns

To better understand people's thought-patterns, I conducted several interviews of individuals. These individuals' identities will not be disclosed and were used only for research. During an interview to better understand the stronghold of thinking negative thoughts, one person shared she'd experienced an unplanned pregnancy while she was going to college. She was young and had great plans for her life. She didn't go to her parents as she didn't want to disappoint them.

She prayed and sought God's help for direction. After feeling some peace within herself, she discussed it with her boyfriend to find out if he would be supportive of her, as she wanted to keep the baby. It was very painful when her boyfriend informed her he didn't want her to keep the baby and wanted her to abort the baby. He would pay for the abortion because he wanted this problem to go away. At that point, she felt hatred toward the man she thought she loved. She had an internal battle because, in good conscience, she wanted to keep the baby, yet he wanted her to abort their baby. She thought she would be able to change his mind, so she continued to see him. Every time they were together, he would tell her he hated the fact she wanted to keep 'it'.

She got upset and decided to abort after her boyfriend pressured and persuaded her to abort the baby if she wanted to keep him. She couldn't explain it, but somehow, she felt the unborn child felt the rejection from the father. She believed the baby actually heard the negative feelings that were discussed about the baby. After much discussion with her boyfriend and with her parents, her final decision was to have the baby. Her boyfriend left her.

The person was very candid when she spoke about her baby and explained that the negative vibes or the negative words spoken over her baby before the baby was born manifested in her child's early life. She worked extra hard to be the best mother she could to her child and gave the baby so much love. She confessed, that even in her womb, she wanted her baby to feel secure and loved, and it was the best thing she did to separate herself and her unborn baby from the baby's father.

Later as the child grew up, she allowed the father to visit, but she refused to let her child be in a negative environment. She explained, that long before she had the baby, she labored in her mind to think through the 'what-if' scenarios in her life. If she had the baby, would she continue college? Would she be able to afford the baby? She went through such a battery of thoughts that she thought she could lose her mind. What she said was helpful to finding a sense of relief was to not allow her mind to explore the unknowns. In other words, she could control herself and she would not allow herself to be bombarded with things she had no control over. This helped her during this dilemma, and when her mind was scattered all over the place, she would pray and put on soft-listening music to ease her mind.

On the contrary, I interviewed another person who'd experienced an abortion and I wanted to find out her thought-patterns during that traumatic time. This person appeared to be very self-confident and had a healthy self-image. She shared during the interview that she was married but they were having marital problems, so she didn't want to bring a child into that environment. She struggled with thoughts of aborting the child or keeping the child. Her mind was so confused, she explained, that she sought professional help to sort out her thought-process. Her mind was racing from one thought to another, and it was uncontrollable. She didn't share her thoughts with her husband because her thoughts were that she would be the parent to raise the child in the event they divorced. She also admitted she was selfish and didn't want the responsibility of being a single parent. Her and her husband did eventually divorce. She's in a relationship now.

Power Talk Segment

We will now discuss the Power Talk segment. I want to use as my reference point for this segment a very vital Scripture that describes just how important it is what we allow to come out of our mouths. In the book of James 3:10: *Out of the same mouth come praise and cursing. My brothers and sisters, this should not be.* Another reminder about what we say comes from Proverbs 18:21: *Death and life are in the power of the tongue; and they that love it shall eat the fruit thereof.*

My main point in this segment is simply to ask you a question: Do you talk to yourself? I'm hoping you say, "Yes, of course, I talk to myself." It's okay to talk to yourself. We will explore why it is so important when we do talk to ourselves that we are saying things to build ourselves up in our inner man, not tearing ourselves down. What we do on the inside, which includes our mind and our hearts, will come out.

Look at the pledge I made to myself many years ago. I have also provided a blank form in the Appendix B. This is a pledge for you, as the reader, if you so feel compelled, to complete, because it's 'normal' for healthy people to talk to themselves.

My Pledge

I, <u>*Mary Segars,*</u> have given myself permission to talk to myself as a way of acknowledging my strengths and encouraging myself to be the best me that God has created. I will only say true things about myself that will encourage me to highlight my strengths and my best attributes that will increase and make me even better. I am confident in my God-given talents, such as a <u>*professional speaker*</u> and <u>*an outstanding teacher*</u>.

If I need to improve in any area of my life, I will be willing to learn new things which will allow me to grow and to be a mature person.

I will be kind to me, and in turn, I will be kind to others. I will take care of myself by allowing my body to rest, eating properly, and maintaining a positive attitude about life. If I am not satisfied with things going on in my life, I have the power to change things in my life.

Mary Segars   April 3, 2001

Name & Date

(Note: This is just a sample I used. Please feel free to modify, add, and change to your liking and wording. After all, it is you talking to you!)

I was fascinated about writing this book about Power Talk several years back, but what really spurred me to do this project was when I witnessed my granddaughter actually talking to herself and to her dolls. When I saw that, I remembered when I was a young girl and I too had that experience, and my daughters loved talking to their dolls, so it motivated me do some research about self-talk and what we say to ourselves. When we were children, if we had an imaginary friend, we would talk to that friend. As children, we don't have all these 'hang ups' as adults do and children aren't inhibited; we do what children do. Then, of course, our parents begin to shape our thinking by telling us all the negative words with the good meanings to protect us. For example, don't go out in the street. Rather than letting the child know, when you go to cross the street, first look both ways. If there is a car coming, you must stop on the curb and wait before you cross the street. Once there are no cars, then and only then, you can cross the street. If you like, I can cross the street with you and we will hold hands as we cross the street. Now I totally understand that would be great in a 'perfect' world, but most parents are multitasking as they instruct their children about crossing the street.

I know for a fact I had a fear or a reverence of my mom when she instructed me to do something, especially when my mother pronounced my entire first, middle, and last name. When I heard my mother say this: "Mary Leola Johnson, you'd better come here right now!" Oh boy, I knew she meant business and I'd just better obey.

As life will have it, we get busy with our lives, making a living and the like. I had really just stopped thinking about the notion of writing the book, but it isn't easy to put something down when you know within your being you must write that book. It was easy for me to find excuses after excuses to delay my writing. It had gotten so bad that I was blaming others for me not finishing my book.

Finally, when my grandson was about eight years old, I walked past his room and his door was slightly open. I heard him talking as if he was rehearsing something. I knocked on his door and he was so into his talking that he didn't hear me knocking, requesting to come into his room. I gently pushed his door further open, and there he was, extending his hands out and reciting Dr. Martin Luther King's speech, *I Have a Dream*. I was in awe because he was really into character with this speech.

I applauded him after he finished and he looked surprised to see me in his room. He invited me to sit down and listen to his speech. He shared that he was going to make his classmates believe he was Dr. Martin Luther King and would sound like him. I sat there and listened and told him how proud I was of him, that he would do the best portrayal of Dr. King. When the actual performance night at his school came, the entire family went to support him. I must admit the entire class did an excellent job, but my grandson was exceptionally great because he'd practiced and he emulated Dr. King. It became crystal clear to me that we do talk to ourselves when I caught him talking to himself.

So, I went back to my computer and started dusting off the pages I'd started so many years ago writing this book. Another reason and incentive to complete my book was because I am finally finishing up with my school work to obtain my doctoral degree from Destiny School of Ministry, and I was reminded I needed to write my dissertation. I just knew my book would be my dissertation. Just sometimes, as life will have it, you recognize it is the right time, and you must seize the moment and opportunity to accomplish two things with one event!

When I worked at GM at the downtown Detroit headquarters, I didn't like to drive downtown in my car, so I decided to 'park and drive' and take the Smart Bus system to work. There were many other people who worked at GM or other companies downtown who'd decided to ride the Smart Bus to commute to their workplaces. Basically, there were many business people riding on the bus. On this one particular day riding to work, there was a lady sitting next to me on the bus. We greeted each other and settled down for the forty-five-minute ride to work. The bus driver called out each stop for the riders' convenience. I was reading a book and she was just enjoying the ride. We were thirty minutes into our ride, and as I turned the page in my book, I heard the lady next to me say something that was inaudible to me. I put my bookmark on the page in my book and looked at the lady.

I finally said to her, "Excuse me, were you talking to me?"

She looked me in my eyes and said, "No, sorry; I was thinking out loud to myself." Then she smiled.

I smiled back and continued to read my book. I knew that lady and she wasn't crazy, but a very astute business lady.

I shared that story with you because, in actuality, we both were talking to ourselves. As I was reading my book, I was speaking the words on the pages of the book to myself. On the other hand, the lady was thinking and speaking to herself out loud. She didn't intend for me to hear what she was thinking and saying to herself, but it came out inadvertently. Haven't you had a similar experience like this? I am sure you have and it is perfectly normal. In fact, it is very encouraging to hear our own voice when we are thinking or reading silently.

If you'll notice on Pie Chart 1 below, where people indicated where they talk to themselves, the location in the car by far outranked any other places. Next time you're driving and you're stopped at a red light, just look over at the driver in the next car and see if they are talking to themselves. Many times when I was talking to myself in my car and I was at a stoplight, I would notice the driver or the passenger in the car next to me looking at me. I'd pretend I was singing along with my radio or CD in my car and wave my hands in the air as if I was singing and couldn't wait until the light turned green. I shouldn't have been embarrassed because a person I didn't know and would probably never see again had seen me talking to myself. If I'd had enough nerve, I should have told them, "It's normal to talk to yourself; perhaps you should try it."

The second place was not so surprising to me because it's one of my favorite places to talk to myself—in the bathroom. There is a mirror in the bathroom and you can look at yourself as you talk to yourself. That's a great place when you are rehearsing a speech or preparing for a job interview. You can see the way your mouth pronounces certain words, etc. You get the point that the mirror can give you a visual of yourself. Sometimes we need to see ourselves as we talk.

Coming in third place was the bedroom, and again, that's understandable as well. As you are getting dressed in the morning, sometimes you're asking yourself, "Where are my shoes?" Or maybe you might say something like this: "No, I don't like this necklace with my dress." Or maybe this: "Oh, I'll wear these earrings instead of these." Trust me, it's okay.

The last location was a bit different to me; well, maybe not—talking to oneself in the closet. It could be a spacious, walk-in closet.

Bar Chart 1 below gives the graphic view that people really do talk to themselves to a tune of 95.3% according to a survey that was conducted. It's quite interesting that the percentage of positive self-talking is lower than the percentage of negative self-talk by 22.1%. Of course, it doesn't surprise me that mostly everyone thinks other people most definitely talk to themselves.

Pie Chart 1
Places Where People Talk to Themselves

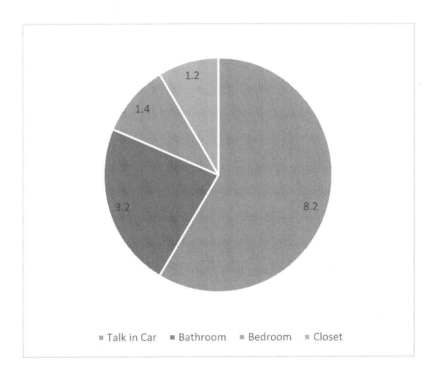

Bar Chart 1
Survey – Do You Talk to Yourself?

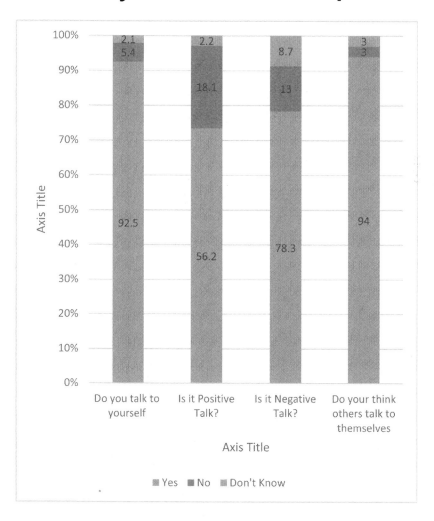

During my research, I searched for people talking to themselves and was very pleasantly surprised to find in the *Elite Daily* publication dated July 9, 2015, an article entitled, *People Who Talk to Themselves Aren't Crazy, They're Actually Geniuses.*[38]. This article indicated that the smartest people on earth talk to themselves. I didn't realize Albert Einstein talked to himself. Visiting the website Einstein.org reports he "use to repeat his sentences to himself softly". The *Quarterly Journal of Experimental Psychology* conducted a study which concluded that talking to yourself makes your brain work more efficiently.[39]

I did a spontaneous survey once just to verify that people really do talk to themselves. A few years back, the film business arrived in the metropolitan Detroit area. I was attending a seminar in a local hotel and I noticed at least three hundred persons waiting in line for an audition. I intentionally stopped to observe the people. I really do enjoy people watching. I've learned so much by watching the dynamics of people interacting with each other and with themselves. Many of the 'soon-to-be-a-star' participants had scripts in their possession. There was so much noise coming from the people that the security guards came over and requested they be quiet because on the other side of the closed doors were people conducting auditions. One very-excited woman in line informed the guard that she was practicing for her audition. He shook his head as if he understood but wanted her to practice her part quietly. It quieted down for a few minutes, then the voices again came up from the crowd practicing their parts for the audition.

It was quite amazing to see so many people talking to themselves all at one time. All of those people were serious about being the next new actor or new actress, and they were doing everything to make that a reality for themselves. Yes, they were talking to themselves to secure the part the producers were looking for. I was almost late for the seminar I was attending because I was so interested in the dynamics of the people talking to themselves! Those people weren't crazy; they wanted to be part of the film industry, and if it required their needing to talk to themselves, so be it. Remind you, they were not talking to each other, which is considered communication, but rather each person was talking out loud to no one but themselves. I was convinced even the more that people really do talk to themselves.

When a person is so captivated by their own thoughts— and in this case, they wanted to make a good impression to the person who could offer them an opportunity to go into the movie business—a person will rehearse and speak to themselves in public! Most people usually they talk to themselves in private because they don't want anyone else around them to hear them talking to themselves.

According to Shad Helmstetter, Ph.D., author of *What to Say When You Talk to Yourself,* explained there are four levels of self-talk. He defines self-talk as a way to override our past negative programming by erasing or replacing it with conscious, positive new direction.[40] It has been proven that most people actually do talk to themselves, and since childhood, we have been programmed to speak negative, mainly because we hear so much negativity.

Once in my group coaching session, the assignment for my clients was to not listen to the news, neither local or national, or read the newspaper. Their assignment was to immerse themselves in listening to music, to concentrate on their breathing, and to think of their good qualities, talents, and gifts. It was amazing when the group session resumed that many enjoyed not being exposed to the negative news on the TV or in the paper. One client indicated he would never listen to CNN again, which he coined as, 'continuous negative news'. That would be eliminated so he could continue with uplifting and encouraging news. I shared with my group that sometimes just a small adjustment in our thinking and speaking can make a momentous difference in our lives.

Further noted, Helmstetter indicated that with self-talk, we will be giving new directions to our subconscious minds by talking to ourselves in a different way, consciously reprogramming our internal control centers with words and statements which are more effective and more helpful to every part of us we would like to improve. Now will this happen overnight? Absolutely not. Just like it took years and years of listening and speaking negative words into our lives, it will take time, work, and dedication to start a new way of talking about ourselves and to ourselves.

My first encounter with the book was when I decided to sell Mary Kay. In fact, I was purchasing the products from a dear friend of mine and I really liked the products. I was her customer for about six months before she approached me about being a Mary Kay distributor. I wasn't interested in selling, as I was working full-time, had a family to see after, and was going to school; no, I just wasn't interested at all. The lady who was selling me the products was a director in Mary Kay, and she was very successful and growing her business. Well, needless to say, she invited me to a meeting, convinced me (I think she really persuaded me) to give this business a try, and said she, personally, would assist me with the business. I joined, and in retrospect, those multi-level business people really know how to push the right emotional button to get the new prospect excited about selling. As I learned more about the business and how to recruit, I found myself at the Red Jacket level, which meant that I had five other distributors under me and my director just knew I would be her next director.

My director wanted her downline (people she'd recruited into the business) to attend this seminar about personal development. She personally paid for this company to come to our office to train her recruits. I invited my five recruits and encouraged them to bring new prospects as well. The seminar was very productive and didn't only talk about selling but also how to improve yourself and be confident within yourself. It was one of the best seminars I've ever attended. The presenter had a book he recommended that every person at the seminar should purchase. We were all so pumped and ready to do almost anything this presenter asked, so I purchased the book. The presenter indicated that, after reading the book, he changed his life and was able to do anything he put his mind to. Of course, the selling part was coming now and he'd sold so many millions of dollars of Mary Kay. I knew it was coming, however, what I took from the seminar was not the selling part, but how I could be better if I talked to myself the 'right' way.

All my life, I've really had a good outlook on life, and for the most part, I am very positive. My sister-in-law once shared with me that, because of my personality, people just naturally gravitated to me. I think she told me, I am not a stranger to anyone. Thinking of that description of me from her made me think, *She's really right on.* I know that is what my parents taught me, to be kind to others and try to see the good in others as well.

There are four levels of self-talk. Beginning with the lowest level, because of the least benefit to the person, as shown on the diagram below, is Negative Acceptance. Many people are living in this level and can't recognize it's dangerous to stay here. Let me give you an example of this level. Have you ever said something like this to yourself: "I'm so stupid?" Or maybe something like this: "This is so dumb of me to do this; yet, I still do it. Go figure." Perhaps you laugh after saying something like that. You are buying into the fact you just called yourself stupid or dumb, and you are okay with that. Many times, we might be around other people when we make a statement like that and your 'friend' might agree with you that you are stupid. That's really so bad, and yet, we accept it.

I can recall once I was in Marshall's shopping and I was in line to purchase my items. I noticed the woman in front of me was searching desperately for something in her purse. The cashier was looking like she was annoyed because, apparently, the woman in front of me didn't have enough money to purchase her items. The next thing I heard out of this woman's mouth was: "Oh, I am an idiot! I left my wallet in my other purse. Oh, what an idiot."

When I heard that woman talking about herself like that, something went off in my mind, and I immediately interrupted her from negative talk to herself. I said, "Excuse me; you are not an idiot just because you left your wallet in your other purse. Don't you ever call yourself that again." She looked at me as if to say, "Mind your own business, lady." I continued and told her, "We all have forgotten something before and that's normal. It is a minor mistake."

The cashier smirked and I looked at her with gleaming eyes as if to say, "You'd better not say a word." Then I asked the woman if she minded if I paid for her items. She looked startled. I could see she was hurting inside because of embarrassment. She started to put back the stuff she had taken out of her purse, blushed, and murmured something to herself. Then she looked at me and said, "No, no, that's not necessary. You don't have to do that."

I held her hand and looked directly in her eyes and said, "Really, it's no problem." I further told her, "I will pay for your items here under one condition." I think that got her attention. She looked and I told her. "If you will never call yourself those degrading names again. Because when you do that, guess what? Your mind will do everything it can to manifest what you've just spoken about yourself. It can't decipher between the good and the bad; it will just try to give you what you say. Will you do that for me?"

She hung her head down and I looked at her until she looked directly at me. I gave the cashier my debit card to pay for the woman's items. When I did that for that woman, it was the best feeling I've experienced in a long time. Now, on the natural side, I was praying she didn't have hundreds of dollars of stuff I'd agreed to pay for. It turned out her items were within my budget and I was able to purchase my own stuff as well. She thanked me so and offered to give me my money back. She gave me her card and I gave her my card as well. I told her this was a 'pay-it-forward' moment for her, and if she had an opportunity, to do the same for someone else. This was for her, regarding her 'self-talk'. That really made my day.

As you see, level 1 is basically negative self-talk. A person will use words like, "I just can't do that!" or "I could never do that." I actually had one of my clients record her day and listen to how many times she used self-badgering or self-assassination words to herself. She was quite surprised how negatively she spoke about herself and others. It was an eye-opening experience for her. The point for that exercise was for her to recognize she was her own worst enemy. This same thing can be true for many of us. It isn't our friends or family who sabotage us, it could very well be ourselves, so we need to be alert and aware to detect what we are saying to ourselves.

Level 2 in self-talk is the level of recognition and need to change. The author indicated that many people are stuck at this level. They acknowledge there is a problem, but will not go beyond that to come up with a resolution. For example, people will say phrases like the following:

"I really need to get more organized."

"I've just got to lose some weight!"

"I really should try to get to work on time."

"I really need to cut down on my smoking."

"I know I should study more."

The author indicated if you hear yourself make statements like those above, he suggested you stop for a moment and complete the sentence. Yes, finish out loud, as you are speaking to your subconscious mind. At this level of self-talk, this actually creates guilt or disappointments. It's like wishing on a dream, then you wake up. The subconscious mind is waiting for you to instruct how you will do the above-mentioned sentences, but at this level, you are satisfied with your inadequacies rather than completing something.

I can remember when I was at this level in my life. In my earlier years, I really enjoyed sewing because it relaxed me, and when I saw the finished product, I was proud I'd made it. At one point in my life, I owned three sewing machines. I taught young ladies how to sew, as I knew it was a lost art the public schools don't teach any more due to budgetary cuts, but sewing can be a necessary, life-saving tool to have in your toolbox. I would tell myself I could sew all my clothes and my daughters' clothes to save money.

Initially, I did sew many items for myself and my girls, but eventually other things took priority, so I hardly sewed anything. However, I told myself, "I need to sew more things for the home, and not just clothes." Or, I told myself, "I should make tablecloths, napkins, etc." Guess what? I didn't do anything. My husband finally told me we were having a garage sale and to set a price for selling my sewing machines. We sold two of my three sewing machines. Can you think of a time when you might have been stuck in this level of self-talk? Take a moment to think if you are currently in this level.

When you think about the first two levels we discussed, those levels really work against us. In level 1, self-talk is strictly negative talking to ourselves and accepting it as factual. Level 2 would be an attempt to recognize change is needed, but we do not make an effort to change—just as I was stuck in level 2 by telling myself what I needed to do, but I didn't have the wherewithal or the power to really do it. I'll go a further step to say I really didn't want to do it, but was just talking about it. The thought came to my mind that 'talk is cheap'. True, but many people live their lives in level 2 and will remain there, as it has become a 'safe haven' or a 'safe place' for them.

At level 3, the author explained this is the first level that works *for* you. Unlike levels 1 and 2, which worked against you, at this level the person is ready to make a change and the self-talk is different because it is in the *present tense*. The tone sounds as if the change has already taken place. Some of the examples of level 3 self-talk could include:

"I no longer have a problem dealing with my co-workers."

"I never eat more than I should and I don't eat after 7 p.m."

When statements like these are made, our subconscious mind is receiving a message to wake up or get moving, and we are making changes. This level of self-talk should be utilized when you have a specific change you want to accomplish in your life. For example, if you are a smoker, you want to talk to your subconscious mind by saying, "I no longer smoke."

Let me pause right here and inform you that neither I nor the author of *What to Say When You Talk to Yourself* is talking about positive thinking at all. Again, self-talk is not magic, hypnosis, mediation, or luck. As I stated before, human beings talk to themselves and that's not a sign of a person being crazy. In fact, if you talk to yourself. you might be considered a genius. This is how our minds work because the subconscious mind will believe anything you tell it long enough and strongly enough.

Level 4 is referred to as 'the better you'. I like to refer to this level as a person sees and speaks to themselves the way God sees and speak of them. I heard myself saying the following statements because they are found in the Bible, which allowed me to use, speak, and believe it for myself:

"I can do all things through Christ Who strengthens me!"

"Greater is He that is inside me, than he who is in the world."

"I am victorious because nothing is impossible with God."

"I walk in perfect health because My Jehovah Rapha healed me."

"No weapons formed against me shall prosper."

At level 4, it is similar to the Maslow's hierarchy of 'self-actualization'. See the chart below depicting the highest level regarding self-confidence and self-esteem. I think it is very similar to the level 4 self-talk, 'the better you'.

Diagram 3
Levels of Self-Talk

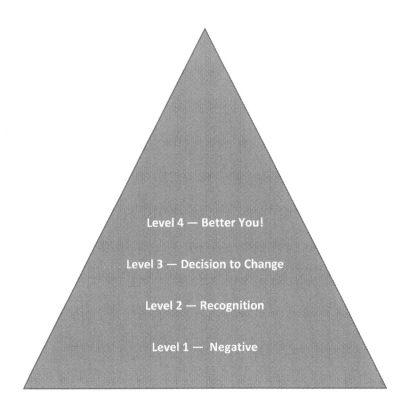

Diagram 4
Maslow's Hierarchy of Needs

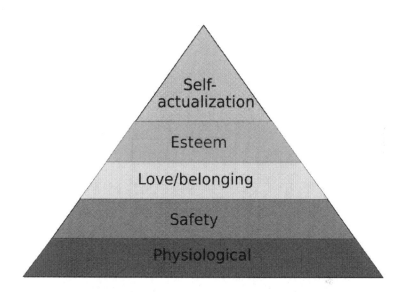

If you still aren't convinced people really do talk to themselves, try this experiment. Next time you are in your waiting room at your doctor or dentist's office with other people there, take a quick look around to see if you notice anyone in the room who might be making an audible sound and no one is talking to them. That could be an indication the person is having a conversation with themselves, then something comes out of their mouth. I'm sure that person doesn't want the other people in the waiting room to hear it, but it just came out. It happens more than we realize. I'm sure it might have happened to you as well. Experts consider talking to oneself as a subset of thinking. You're actually having a conversation with yourself. I'm confessing I do talk to myself!

I've covered self-talk that is positive and self-talk that is negative. Satan not only self-talked to himself, but he talked to God about what he had thought about for a long time. See the reference in Power Thought about what satan thought and eventually spoke to God.

God talked to Himself when He spoke in the beginning:

Genesis 1:3 (KJV): *And God said, "Let there be light; and there was light."*

Genesis 1:6: *And God said, "Let there be a firmament in the midst of the waters, and let it divide the waters from the waters."*

Genesis 1:11: *And God said, "Let the earth bring forth grass, the herb yielding seed, and the fruit tree yielding fruit after his kind, whose seed is in itself, upon the earth; and it was so."*

Genesis 1:26: *And God said, "Let us make man in Our image, after Our likeness: and let them have dominion over the fish of the sea, and over the fowl of the air, and over the cattle, and over all the earth, and over every creeping thing that creepeth upon the earth."*

Genesis 1:28: *And God said unto them, "Be fruitful, and multiply, and replenish the earth, and subdue it: and have dominion over the fish of the sea, and over the fowl of the air, and over every living thing that moveth upon the earth."*

This is about a person's daily Affirmative Therapy! This is basically doing a daily dose of affirming yourself, your life, and what you want to happen in your life. We really do need to do this. An affirmation is a phrase that can help you invite in positivity and self-care to your daily life. Affirmations help you focus on what you want to draw into your life and can give you something to hang on to when you're having a particularly difficult day.

Let's talk about daily Affirmative Therapy. If we really think about this seriously, we already have a daily confession. This could be our daily prayer. This is a time we speak honestly and openly before our Almighty God! There's no hiding from God because He knows all things. Many times in our prayer time with God, we are speaking His Word back to Him and proclaiming His promises in our lives. We're thanking Him for His loving kindness towards us, and we come with a grateful heart. In one form or another, that's our Prayer Therapy, if you will allow me to call it that to make a point.

Typically, after that, we're on our way, without speaking to ourselves about how we will act or respond to our day. This is what I'm calling our Affirmative Therapy. The Bible tells us to call those things that aren't as though they were. Let's say, for example, in your workplace you are interacting with a person who has a very bad attitude and poor work ethic. You have already prayed to the Lord, and now it's like reminding yourself who you are in God.

In the book of James, it tells us to be a doer of the Word and not a hearer only. For if any be a hearer of the Word and not a doer, he is like unto a man beholding his natural face in the glass (mirror), for he beholds himself, and goes his way, and straightway forgets what manner of man he was. But whosoever looks into the perfect law of liberty, and continues therein, he being not a forgetful hearer, but a doer of the Word, this man shall be blessed in his deed.

I think many times, we forget who we really are in God. That's why I practice saying to myself what the Word of God says about believers. Let's say, for example, you are working with a colleague who does not know the Lord and is doing what the world does best—which is the opposite of what true a disciple does: obeys God's Word at all times. Anyway, the coworker, who has really wracked your nerves by coming in late and leaving early, may not do their work; however, you have already spoken to yourself that: "I am a very productive worker," and, "All I do is for the glory of God." You've told yourself you will always conduct yourself in a very professional manner and you fully understand that promotions are from the Lord. By having a mindset like that, your mind is settled and your heart is fixed to be the best you can be. Trust me, rewards will come to you because you are not moved by what others do or don't do.

I'm always reminding myself and I share this with my clients: It is a full-time job making sure *my life* is tight and right! That doesn't mean not to be concerned for others, but don't get into others' affairs, because you are making sure that you, as an individual, are doing what you are supposed to be doing in your life.

This reminds me of the orientation on an aircraft. I'm sure you have been on a plane, and before the plane took off to your destination, all the passengers had to give attention to the flight attendant's instructions of what was expected of the passengers during the flight in the event an emergency arises. They ensured all passengers were aware of the exits on the aircraft. They reminded us to keep our seatbelts on unless the pilot instructed otherwise. We were told about the flotation devices on the aircraft. Most importantly, the passengers were informed that, in the event there was a loss of altitude, the plane would disperse an oxygen mask for each passenger. Place the mask over your nose and mouth first, and if you have a child or someone depending on you for safety, then put their mask over their nose and mouth next. It is important because if we don't take care of ourselves first, we would be unable to take care of others. That same principle is applicable where we need to make sure we are doing what God told us to do before we start to think what someone else isn't doing.

I would like to share how I had to talk to myself when I worked for a self-centered person. I had to really talk to myself and encourage myself because I knew I was there for an assignment and a purpose. I can remember telling the Lord I wanted to learn my lesson quickly and to keep me moving on to the next assignment. At first, I thought God was deaf because I wanted to get out of that area of work. Sometimes in life, we might have to take a detour and I thought this was an unnecessary detour (this job) because it wasn't in the discipline for which I'd gone to school. I thought this area was demeaning to me. It seemed like I was there forever before I recognized it was my attitude, my thinking-pattern that was causing me to stay there longer than I needed. God was waiting for me to change my mindset.

I've learned that some things in my life were basically because of me and not because of God. He reminded me that He is Almighty and that my mind had not been renewed. My mind was filled with my own frustrations and misunderstanding. As a background, my thinking was narrow-minded and self-absorbed. At the time, I couldn't recognize that and I used the blame game. I would think and say things like, "I'm still in this department because I'm black." And things like, "The company needs a 'minority' on this staff." There was some truth in that statement, and I carried that negative thought and spoke those negative things to some of my colleagues—colleagues who probably didn't think that way—and ignited those thoughts to enter their minds. Just like being positive is contagious, so negative and pessimistic thinking can be contagious and dangerous. The Word of God tells us that faith comes by hearing (I'll leave the hearing the Word of God part out). The more we talked about the unfair treatment, the more the anger was building up within the black workers.

Over a course of months, we had so worked ourselves up that we were beginning to hate our jobs and that 'attitude' was showing up in our demeanor. We wouldn't speak to people on our floor. I really didn't recognize the person I was becoming, but it was easy as we got 'caught up' in the negativity of it all. It is so vivid, as if it was yesterday, but this happened years ago (twenty-plus). We were at lunch and really bashing our employer. Suddenly, as I began to agree we should perhaps seek an attorney and file a racial discrimination case against our company, the Holy Spirit wouldn't let me speak a word. Everyone was looking at me and waiting for me to continue with the bashing. Even when I tried to speak, I just couldn't say a word. From the outside, it looked like I'd lost my thought or something, but on the inside, the Holy Spirit had quieted me so I could hear Him speaking and to say the right thing. I can remember the Holy Spirit saying softly, "Don't say that because you are not telling the truth. You are being deceived, so stop it right now." I was thinking, *Am I having an out-of-body experience like Paul mentioned,* but no, I knew deep within me this was not right.

They kept looking at me, then another coworker began to speak negatively about our employer and I just sat there. The others also talked about how they hated this company. Then the Holy Spirit prompted me, and I was instructed to leave the table and remove myself from them. I tried to excuse myself, but I just got up and left. I didn't look back at them as I went to a conference room and closed the door behind me. When I entered the room, I began to weep and asked God for forgiveness for having the wrong thoughts and to fill me up with his wisdom. I cried out for His guidance, then I was silent. The remainder of my lunch was spent with God. It didn't matter that I was at work; I needed direction from God.

For the next couple of days, I didn't go to lunch with my coworkers. However, a week later, I had lunch with them again. At the outset, I shared with them that I wanted to apologize for my wrong attitude and the negative and harmful talking I had done with them. It was a time for confessing to them that, as a Christian, it wasn't right to stir up this kind of confusion which could lead to other things. Some understood and there were others who thought it wasn't necessary to apologize because, "You are human and you are entitled to feel negative towards the company." I told them I wasn't entitled to have these wrong and negative feelings when I serve a great and mighty God, and that wasn't a good presentation of a great God!

It didn't matter whether they understood or not; I knew for myself I had to get it right with God. My relationship with God is so much more important than my coworkers having lunch with me. I really believe by me taking that stance for God and being right, as far as my thoughts, my feelings, and my actions, really demonstrated to my coworkers that God is real in my life. In fact, one woman I'm still very much friends with even today made a commitment for God and is living her life to please Him. My thoughts were to not be a stumbling block but to be a conduit for others to see God in me and to want to make Him Lord of their lives. I've realized when we yield to God in our thoughts, He will reward those who diligently seek Him.

Back to this department I once hated. I had to change my mind about the place. It started with a decision I made back in that conference room. Once the decision was made, it was the work that followed that decision. I told myself every morning, my God has provided this job for me and I'm thankful for my coworkers. The decision and the confession I made daily allowed me to change my attitude and disposition about that job. It seemed like my boss had changed, but in reality, I was the one who had changed. It was like when I bought a new car and it seemed like I saw more cars like mine. The truth was, there were always cars like mine, but I became more aware since I now had that car as well. It's the awareness that makes us 'wake up' to something that were always there. It was true with my working in that department. It seemed like the people had changed, but because I was willing to change my mindset, that afforded me to see from a new and positive perspective.

I worked in that department for several more years. I learned so much about algorithms, creditworthiness, and so many other new and exciting things I would have never experienced or learned if I hadn't been in that department. I saw new people come and go, but I wasn't focused on that. When I wasn't expecting or thinking of transfer or promotion, it happened, and I knew it was the right timing, as I was emotionally, mentally, and spiritually ready for the next level of promotion in my life. It wasn't just the job; it was the totality of my life that elevated me for the next stage in my life.

Another time in my life when I had to change my mindset was after I retired from General Motors Headquarters after thirty years. I inquired of the Lord what was the next chapter in my life because, retiring from one position, I knew I would be recharging for something different. When I was younger, I had briefly thought it would be great to be a public servant to the people, and my thinking was to be in the political arena. My pastor was involved in the political arena, serving a community on the city council, and she always encouraged others to consider that platform, as God's people need to be in that arena to represent God.

After much prayer and consideration, I took a leap of faith and did a preliminary feasibility study with my closest friends and family members. My family and friends were very encouraged that I would pursue this avenue, and they were going to support me if I wanted to go after it. At our first official 'campaign meeting' at my house, I had my family and friends rally together a strategy plan. One caveat my husband gave me was, I was entering one of the most vicious areas, but no manner what, he would support and pray for me during this endeavor.

I decided to run for the City Clerk position. After obtaining the forms to have my name on the ballot, we went quickly to the residents who resided in my community to sign my petition so I could have my name on the ballot. The team agreed to take forms and obtain signatures. We were at the supermarkets, standing outside the library, going to the neighborhood associations' meetings, and actually going door-to-door requesting signatures. Trust me, I really think we received more 'no' responses initially than 'yes' responses. Our mindsets had to be 'don't give up' because people will tell us no. I know at every meeting we had, we prayed and recited our slogan: "We're in it to win it!" We were pumped up with victory in our hearts and minds so we wouldn't be too traumatized by rejection. I'm not saying it was easy; we had to prevail and be consistent with our thought-patterns.

My campaign manager was so strategic and very positive. When I wanted to throw in the towel and call it off, she was the strong tower to remind me why we were doing it and that the benefit would be for the people. She had me to write down 'why' I wanted to run for this public office; that assignment allowed me to think through the process. I jotted down a few thoughts and she really challenged me to define each reason, because if my 'why' wasn't clear to me and resonant with me, I couldn't expect the followers to support me. I think that was much harder for me than actually running for the office, but I really appreciated her for giving me the assignment to do the critical thinking. She informed me she didn't want to waste her time or my time if we didn't understand why we were doing this whole political thing. Talk about a wakeup call for me! It required me to pull on all my thinking muscles to establish my 'why', which in turn, catapulted the team by knowing my stance on the issues. My caption for this segment is from this quote:

> "You can't spell challenge without change.
> If you're going to rise to the challenge,
> you have to be prepared to change,"
> by Becky Johnen.

During this entire process of campaigning, I really learned something about myself. It is much more than just thinking the way God wants us to think. I had to also perform what I was saying and thinking. My campaign manager estimated we walked to and knocked on approximately four thousand doors. That was amazing to me because she'd strategized how we could touch people in our community because I was a newcomer to this political arena and people needed to know something about me.

One of my relatives personally knew someone in another municipality in the same position I was running for and invited me to meet with that person. That was one of the highlights during this time for me. This person was very professional and carefully advised me to just state my position, what I would bring to the position, and how the residents in my community would benefit if they voted for me. She stressed it wasn't necessary to bring up my opponent's record or position. That was very helpful to me in focusing my mindset on our campaign stance.

As we were developing my campaign signs, it was a thought from our minds onto paper, the sign company designed it, then it was a reality! I kept one of my signs as a reminder. The sign made the very thought I wanted to run for public office such a reality when I saw: *Vote for Mary Segars, City Clerk!* (See Appendix E for a picture of the yard sign.)

Once our family was driving around the city and my grandson shouted out, "THERE'S MY GRANDMA'S NAME. I REALLY LIKE THAT SIGN!" When he shouted that out, my heart was singing on the inside. It was clear politics can be unfair because some of my signs were destroyed on purpose. With my mindset, I understood that was all part of the campaign race, so we just had to replace the signs. There was no need to hold any animosity because we didn't actually know who had destroyed the signs.

Once my campaign manager reminded me we had to develop 'tough skins' and have a strong mind to run this campaign. The verity of her words gave us strength for the many fundraisers we had to support the campaign. We had bowling events and 'meet the candidate' events. When asking people for funds, we developed a strong constitution because we were ready for the negative, but continued until we obtained our financial goal.

As my campaign manager prepared me for the debate, it was very demanding on my mind. She wanted me to think like the people I would be serving, so it was necessary to talk to the residents and find out what they wanted in a public servant. What were their expectations and how could a public servant better serve them? This kind of thinking afforded me the opportunity to do role-playing to analyze the problems and establish workable solutions. We would spend hours after hours reviewing, rehearsing, and evaluating. That was a very valuable time for me and for my campaign workers. They were representing me out in the public, so we wanted to have the same theme and the same mindset when we encountered the public. The team needed to know my thoughts clearly so they could relay them to others in the community.

At the actual debate, I was prepared and that venue required that I think fast on my feet. Sure, preparation is definitely needed, but you can't anticipate all the kinds of questions the residents will pose at an event like a debate. The organization sponsoring the debate allowed questions from the audience, so the candidates needed to have a broad understanding about the position we were seeking in the election as well as the city's general policies and procedures. This was much more advanced than the high school debates I'd enjoyed many years ago. However, this kind of debate permitted me go into my repertoire from my experiences in the corporate world, as well as my life experiences, to provide answers to the questions.

I was always reminded it is very difficult to go against an incumbent, especially if that person has had that position for many years. Although I didn't make it past the primary election, it was an experience I'm glad I attempted to fulfill my goal. It was a pleasant surprise when the incumbent informed me I'd conducted a very good and fair campaign.

Again, that campaign experience elevated me to another thinking level as far as attempting to reach a goal. Yes, at times it was frustrating, but that process gave me ample time to renew my mind, refocus my mind, and sharpen my thinking mechanics. It really stretched my thinking to be more positive even in a bad situation. I've tried to find the good and the benefit I received by going through it.

Through the campaign experience, I'm convinced this is not my platform, but I'm glad I did it, and I can cross that off my bucket list of things I thought I wanted to do and pursue. I related my campaign experience to a Bible story we're familiar with. It is when all the disciples were in the boat and Jesus appeared to them. They thought it might be a ghost and Jesus assured them not to be afraid. However, Peter responded to Jesus and requested to come onto the water. Jesus simply told to Peter, "Come." Peter stepped outside the boat and attempted to meet Jesus on the water. I don't think he regretted that he attempted to meet Jesus on the water, because he thought he could, even though he became distracted with the waves and his focus turned to him drowning (Matthew 14:22-32). I attempted and I have no regrets because the lessons I learned are immeasurable. This whole scenario makes me think about the Scripture in Proverbs 18:16: *A man's gift maketh room for him, and bringeth him before great men. (KJV)*

So, if you are experiencing something in your life and it isn't going as you thought or expected, take that as a learning tool for yourself. Here's another quote I'd like for you to think about, as I had to pull the quote out to remind me: "I never lose. Either I win or I learn."

An Exercise for Seminar Participants

One of my sessions at the seminar emphasized the point of how powerful negative thinking and negative speaking can impact your attitude, your temperament, and of course, your mind. For this exercise, I shared this was just a demonstration and needed someone to volunteer to be the person who would receive and hear one negative remark from me. I had one person agree to the exercise and volunteer to sit in a chair. I first asked the person to share one goal with the group. In this particular session, the person shared she wanted to start her own weave, wig, and hair business. I requested that the other participants clap to show their enthusiasm about this person's goal.

Then I went up to the participant sitting in the chair who had just shared her goal and said the following to her: "Now you know you're just dreaming because you will never have your own business. You didn't even go to school and you don't have a degree. What kind of knowledge do you have about having your own business? Right, no knowledge. You'd better go and find a job in a wig shop and be happy with your life."

The next part to this exercise was to have twelve-to-fifteen other participants come up to the willing participant in the chair and all give positive statements. The first participant said, "You can have your own business and begin now." The second participant informed her, "If you have the desire and passion and the will to have your business, you must do it." The third participant stated, "You can do all things through Christ and He will strengthen you."

The fourth participant said very adamantly and pointed her finger in the face of the participant sitting in the chair, "If you don't start your business, you will regret it for the rest of your life. You'd better get started and don't let anyone or anything stop you!"

After all twelve participants spoke to the person sitting in the chair, and after each encouragement and each positive word was spoken to her, you could actually see how her countenance changed. It was amazing to see her face start to smile and it was reflected in her body movements. She was totally elated and her attitude was moved by the positive confirmations.

After the completed exercise, the willing participant came back up to the front, and I wanted the participants to evaluate the exercise. I asked her the following question: "How did you feel when I made that negative statement to you?"

She told the group: "I felt terrible. It was as if someone had kicked me in the stomach and I was in pain. I was crushed and began to doubt my goal and my plan to start a new business."

Next, I wanted her to share with the group how she felt after she heard the twelve positive statements.

She began to smile and said: "Initially, I thought the first couple of positive statements were to pacify me, but after hearing more and more of those words of encouragement, they helped me to regain my strength and my thoughts. Each statement helped me find my power to pursue my goals. They resonated within me because this is my goal. It seemed like each positive statement, along with the smiles and sincerity, lifted my spirit. Afterwards, I had the determination to fulfill my plans."

What she said next was interesting because her body language was very congruent with what she said. "After about the tenth or eleventh positive statement, I felt like I became more and more certain I would accomplish my goals, and I don't care what others think. This is my life. It was like I could see my business!"

We all applauded the willing participant and then I shared with the group that one, only one, negative statement we hear or speak to ourselves can deter us from pursuing our goals or our plans. Therefore, it usually takes ten-to-fifteen positive statements to overcome that one negative thought. The group witnessed that this exercise had some validity when they saw how she changed her whole body gestures as she continued to hear and agree with the positive statements.

Again, we are so use to talking negatively and we somewhat accept it because we've been programmed to negativity. However, we need to demolish the negative with many, many positive reinforcements. That example at the seminar was so impactful to the participants on so many levels. After the session, so many expressed to me they hadn't fully realized how important it was to think as well as speak positively to themselves.

I want to give a personal testimony about when I really became a prolific Power Talker. This was when I had the opportunity to make my words into action. Back in 2013, I had a medical challenge and how it occurred was nothing but a miracle from God.

All my adult life, I have been in excellent health condition, and in my annual physicals, my doctor would only encourage me to lose five-to-seven pounds. I started out cutting carbs, and since I retired in 2008, I walk three times a week in the mall with other retirees and friends. I've even joined a group called T.O.P.S. which stands for Taking Off Pounds Sensibly. We met once a week and had to weigh-in with a report of if we'd lost, stayed the same, or gained weight. We discussed how to lose weight, portion sizes and control, and exercise. Because there were no consequences if we gained weight—like pay a penalty or anything—there really wasn't an incentive to lose weight. We each had to give a 'pep' talk about how we lost weight. One of my presentations was on not to compete with each other, but to compete with yourself and your own weight. It starts with your mindset about losing weight. I encouraged my fellow T.O.P.S. members to write down their desired weight, goals of how they would obtain that desired weight, then implement their plan. After a while, the meeting became a social outing, so I decided to leave the group.

In the fall of 2013, I was driving home and had stopped at a red light. As I was waiting, a car driving quite fast was making a very wide right turn and ran right into my car. I couldn't go anywhere, and it was like in slow motion when I saw that car hurtle into my car. The impact of the accident jerked my head, my glasses went flying off, and I gripped the steering wheel and cried out, "Jesus!" The driver jumped out her car and her passenger also jumped out to see if I was all right. I was stunned because, in all my years of driving, I had never had a car accident! I slowly got out my car, and my front end was totally smashed in and the engine was smoking.

There was another car on my right also stopped at the red light and the driver came to assist me as I was really dazed. I tried to find my glasses and noticed the other driver who had witnessed the accident dialed 911. I heard the ambulance and I couldn't find my purse which had fallen under the front passenger seat. This woman was like an angel on assignment and she came to assist me. She was able to get my glasses and my purse. I called my husband and my daughter and told them to meet me at the hospital as I had been in an accident.

It turned out the young girl was learning to drive, and her uncle (he had one arm) was teaching her how to drive and how to make turns! I was thinking I was at the wrong place at the wrong time but, in actuality, I really was at the right place at the right time. My car was totaled and my insurance company paid me so I was able to buy a new car.

The EMT placed me in a neck brace and I lay on a back board as they put me in the ambulance truck. They rushed me to the hospital as my neck and back were in pain. Riding in an ambulance is not fun at all because you can feel every crevice in the road. Once I arrived at the hospital, my family met me there, as well as my pastor. They took x-rays of my neck and my back. My left arm had turned black and blue, perhaps from holding the steering wheel so tight at the time of the impact.

All this time, I was praying to the Lord, and as I stated above, when the car crashed into my car, I called out Jesus' name. Sometimes just calling upon His name is what is needed. As we waited for the results of the x-rays, the ER doctor didn't see any breakage of my bones but knew I would feel pain for the next couple of days from the crash. He recommended I take aspirins for the pain and to seek my physician within a couple of days. I was so sore and in so much pain for the next several days, and I did schedule an appointment to see my internist.

My doctor had received my x-rays as he was affiliated with the hospital to which I'd gone. He informed me he noticed a nodule on my left thyroid, and he wanted me to see an endocrinologist and schedule a biopsy on the nodule. I asked him to recommend an endocrinologist and he did. I questioned him very thoroughly about the nodule and he explained it was a lump, swelling, or a growth on the thyroid gland. He further explained that usually the nodules are non-cancerous. I also went on MD.com to read more about nodules. I scheduled an appointment for my biopsy my doctor had recommended.

I was feeling very confident that all was well and this is just a procedure I was going through. I had the biopsy and the results would be provided to the endocrinologist who had performed the procedure as well as my main (internist) doctor. After three days, I received a call from the endocrinologist's office and was informed that the biopsy was normal and there wouldn't be any need for any other tests and/or procedures. That was great news to me, so I carried on with my life.

Two days later, I received a call from the endocrinologist's office, and this time it wasn't the office clerk, it was the doctor. He explained that the call I'd received the other day was incorrect and he had the correct results now. (Immediately, my mind doubted what the doctor was able to tell me because I had recently read an article that exposed how doctors would tell patients they have a disease, and in reality, the patients don't have it. However, the doctors want to conduct surgery and collect money from the insurance companies.) My doctor went on to explain that the results of my biopsy indicated the nodule was approximately one inch in diameter, and it looked 'suspicious' and should be removed. I wanted him to define 'suspicious'. He went on to tell me it couldn't be determined if it was cancerous, but being that size, it really should be removed. I requested a copy of the biopsy report to be mailed to me so I could review it with my husband. I received the report within a couple of days and immediately scheduled an appointment with another endocrinologist to obtain another opinion. In the meanwhile, I was thinking all sorts of things, but my mind went back to the Word of God. I quoted out loud all my healing scriptures; I meditated on those scriptures.

I went to the second doctor for his opinion and the results were pretty much the same as the first diagnosis. I went back to my internist and it seemed like he was rushing me to make a decision about the surgery to remove the nodule from my thyroid. I informed him I would talk it over with my husband and we would pray about this surgery because I wasn't ready to make a decision right then. He let me know I shouldn't take too long to take care of this medical matter.

What I allowed my mind to do was to not think about this situation, then I wouldn't have to deal with it. My subconscious mind told me to do some additional research. I delayed thinking about it; however, I continued to do research on the internet about thyroid cancer. The second doctor I went to had been highly recommended to me by my husband's doctor, so I scheduled an appointment to discuss the next steps after about three months of dealing with the delayed-thinking process.

This doctor recommended a surgeon who had performed over two hundred thyroid operations and he was a specialist in this area. I agreed to meet with this surgeon, and he had my entire medical chart and the results of the biopsy. He thoroughly explained everything to my husband and me. He gave us pamphlets about the thyroid and had drawings of what he would do in the surgery. He informed us of the possibility that, if he went in to remove the left thyroid and the growth looked like it might have started to grow on the right thyroid, he would have to remove the entire thyroid. He elaborated that, if he removed either a part of or the entire thyroid, I would have to take medication.

After that consultation, the doctor wanted to schedule the surgery, but I insisted I would call his office when I was ready to schedule the surgery. My husband and I prayed together, and we decided I would go through with the surgery. The surgery was scheduled for the next week. My family members were informed and they all came down to pray with me. It was strange that I wasn't nervous, as I felt a peace with God, and we prayed for the surgeon and the surgical team. The surgery went very well, and the doctor informed my family he had removed the entire thyroid and would have the pathology report within a couple of days.

While I was in the recovery room coming out of the anesthesia, I didn't feel any pain in my throat even when I reached for my neck and felt the bandage. When I looked up, my husband and my daughters were in the recovery room with me. I guess I was still very groggy, but one look at them and I smiled. I attempted to speak, but I couldn't hear my voice and they indicated to me I didn't have to try to speak now. I closed my eyes, then I heard my sister's voice. I looked up again and saw my niece and brother-in-law. They smiled and encouraged me. Next, I was moved into my room, and the doctor came in and informed me I should not cough for the next couple of days. It was hard because all I wanted to do was cough. What was required for me to do was talk to myself so I could get through this post-surgery. Speaking God's Word in my mind was constant and continuous all during my three days in the hospital.

During this whole time of post-surgery, my family was there and encouraging me that all was well. When I finally spoke, my voice was different. It sounded very deep and it was strange to hear my own voice. My doctor explained that my normal voice would probably come back in a couple of weeks. When I went back to the doctor's office for a two-week checkup, my voice was still deep and so different. At this point, my prayers were very specific and detailed, and I requested a full voice restoration. It was different, but somehow, I liked the soft-spoken voice. I would be very self-conscious when I was in a crowd and the voices were very loud, and I sounded like I was whispering. It became very frustrating for me, and as I was praying to the Lord and in my quiet time waiting to hear from God, it was so clear I was hearing from God and it resonated in my spirit: "You've asked Me to change and mold you, and it's not what you expected, so you want to complain. This is your new voice and I will give you my Word to speak it to the world." Prior to this confirmation Word from the Lord to me, I would always apologize to people about my voice. The Lord informed me,

"No more. You don't need to apologize for something I'm doing in your life."

Once, I was at a gathering and as long as I was talking one-on-one with a person, it went well. It was when I was in a crowd or group of talkers that it seemed my voice diminished even more. A person I didn't know very well came up to me, and she mentioned to me that her sister had had her thyroid removed and her normal voice came back within a couple of days. I thanked her for sharing the information with me even though I hadn't solicited the information. Then I walked away from her before I said something else to her that would not have been nice. That comforted me so in my mind and the way I thought and the way I spoke. It was so refreshing to know God is totally in control and all I need to do is trust in Him for all things.

One month after my surgery, it was necessary for me to go to the Nuclear Medicine department so the doctors could determine if the surgeon had removed all the thyroid and what was the level of iodine remaining in my thyroid area. I had to go on a low-iodine diet on which I had to eat certain foods; then it was scheduled for me to meet the specialists to administer nuclear radiation to remove any microscopic pieces remaining. I spoke very positively that, "Everything has been removed and I'm believing God."

After the screening, the doctor showed me that everything had been removed and it would be necessary to have this screening again in one year. Every time I went to the speech therapist and the ear, nose, and throat specialist, I spoke my confession of "I'm healed". The nuclear medicine specialist gave a report to my main doctor and I requested a copy of the report for my medical records. To my amazement, the report stated, "It was a pleasure to work with this patient as she is very knowledgeable and astute about her medical condition and remedies available. Her positive disposition is very encouraging and she has taken responsibility for her health."

One year after my surgery, I had to retake the nuclear radiation treatment again to view if there were any changes. I spoke to myself that my God is my healer and I'm totally healed. I spoke it, then I declared I was healed. When I went in for the radiation this time, the results were excellent, and I was told I didn't have to come back for five years!

I am a prolific Power Talker because I know, for me to overcome anything in my life, my family, or my health, etc., it is necessary for me to have power thoughts, to align my words with my thoughts, and to be consistent with God's Word.

So, are you a Power Talker? Do you speak life into your situations? Do you meditate on what God has proclaimed in your life? Are you expecting that God's Word will not return to Him void, but it will accomplish all that He sent it do?

Happy Power Talk! Be a great Power Talker which starts with your power thoughts!

Next Steps

The following is my sincere desire for you, the reader, to do after reading this book:

1. Be a power thinker who wants to be associated with other like-minded thinkers.

    a. Iron sharpens iron.

2. Be a firm thinker about your life, your family, and your decisions that will benefit you for the better.

    a. Develop critical-thinking and deep-diving-thinking skills.

    b. Allow the Holy Spirit to assist your thinking.

    c. Pray to have a mind like Christ.

3. Renew your mind and allow God's Word to transform (change) you.

4. The Power Talk starts with Power Thoughts.

    a. Begin Affirmative Therapy, where you're speaking to yourself about your strengths, your gifts, and your talents.

    b. Allow your gifts to lead you to your purpose.

    c. Walk in your purpose, your anointing.

    d. Seek God's Word as the basis for your Power Talk.

Affirmative Therapy

This segment is designed to help you implement a daily practice of thinking and speaking God's Word, and like I tell my clients, practice makes better. The more we do something, the better we become. There is something about allowing your ear to hear your voice speaking that will digest in your mind and in your heart (spirit) to completely resonate within you— to resonate within your soul, to totally resonant within your heart (spirit). Just like David declared: "I had to encourage myself in the Lord."

We shouldn't expect encouragement to come from anyone outside of ourselves. Don't misunderstand, you very well could receive encouragement from outside sources, which could include your spouse, your church, your family, and friends; however, if those other sources do not provide the encouragement you were expecting, remember what Psalm 63:4 tells us: *My expectation is from You (God).* We can't blame anyone else because the Bible tells us in I Peter 1: *I've given you everything pertaining to life and godliness.*

We don't have an excuse and we can't blame others. We are admonished to study to show ourselves approved by God (not men). (II Timothy 2:15)

I've called this process Affirmative Therapy because it's just like, if you have a knee replacement, after surgery it will be necessary to go to physical therapy for several months to acclimate the new knee to your body. The physical therapy will exercise the new knee and cause the muscles to be strengthened. Likewise, the Affirmative Therapy will build up your Power Talk, which begins with your Power Thoughts, to develop a winning strategy for your life.

None of us are promised a rose garden in life; in fact, with roses there will be thorns! So, to build our immune systems in our minds and spirits, it is necessary to practice Affirmative Therapy. As we have discovered, we actually do talk to ourselves, and it's vital we say the correct 'self-talk'. What we say to ourselves can cause victory or can cause disaster. It is strictly up to you what you want to say and do for your life.

Below are merely examples, but I promise, once you begin your daily Affirmative Therapy, you will develop your own for yourself.

Monday: This is a brand-new day that my Lord has made, and I will rejoice and I will be glad in it. Whatever comes to me that will attempt to move me from my space of rejoicing, this is being served as notice: It won't happen today. My mind is settled in this position. Not today!

Tuesday: Today, I've received God's mercies that are new every morning. By receiving His mercies, there will be plenty of opportunities for me to also extend mercies to people I'll encounter during the course of my day. It will be a joy to 'pay it forward' with His mercy because it endures forever. There will be no need for me to judge anyone, but use me Lord to be a conduit so others will experience Your love through me.

Wednesday: I'm so grateful for Your loving kindness You have shown me, Oh Lord, so grateful for Your power, very grateful for Your goodness. You alone are worthy of all praise, all glory, and all worship. It's Your Name that I'll laud forevermore.

~~~~~~~~~~~~

I trust you are getting the idea that each day there can be an affirmative statement or a phrase to speak out loud to yourself. It's like taking your daily vitamins!

Here are a few I repeat to myself everyday:

1. I have chosen to be happy today and every day.

2. I am a doer of the Word and not a hearer only.

3. Because I believe in Christ, I am daily renewing my mind to have the mind of Christ.

4. This is going to be a great day for me and everyone I come into contact with today!

5. I will be the best me today!

6. This is a brand-new day, and I have another chance to impact someone else's life!

7. I am learning how to release my stress because I am too blessed to be stressed!

8. I can't take life so seriously!

9. I am learning to laugh more and more. I even laugh at myself!

10. It is perfectly normal for me to talk to myself as I will encourage myself. I can't expect others to do that for me. It's like taking my daily vitamins!

11. I've learned to love me for me.

12. I'm discovering more about me as I allow the Holy Spirit to reveal me to me!

13. I will denounce all negative thoughts concerning me and my family!

14. It's very therapeutic to talk to myself.

15. I am too blessed to be stressed or depressed!

APPENDIX A

Footnotes

1. Thomas Nelson Holy Bible, New King James Version, Copyright @ 1982.

2. Quest Study Bible, NIV Quest Study Bible, Copyright @ 1994, 2005 by Zondervan.

3. Quest Study Bible.

4. Quest Study Bible.

5. Quest Study Bible.

6. John McDowell, *Building Your Self-Image,* 1986 (Living Books edition), Tyndale House Publishers, Inc., Wheaton, Illinois, 3-6.

7. McDowell, 11-17.

8. Quest Study Bible, Ephesians 1:6-8, Romans 8:1, 38.

9. Quest Study Bible, Romans 5:10, 2 Corinthians 5:18-19, Colossians 1:21-22, Hebrews 10:19-22

10. Quest Study Bible, Matthew 20:28, 1 Timothy 2:5-6

11. Quest Study Bible, Ephesians 1:13-14, Colossians 1:14, Titus 2:14, Hebrews 9:12, 1 Peter 1:18.

12. Quest Study Bible, Romans 8:29, 2 Timothy 2:19.

13. Quest Study Bible, Romans 8:30, Ephesians 1:4, 1 Peter 2:9.

14. Quest Study Bible, Romans 3:23-26, Romans 5:1, Romans 8:1, 30.

15. Quest Study Bible, Romans 15:7, Ephesians 1:4-6, 1Peter 2:10.

16. Quest Study Bible, Romans 5:8-10, 7:13-25; Ephesians 2:1-20, Colossians 1:15.

17. Quest Study Bible, Psalm 89:3, 1 Peter 2;3, 9.

18. Quest Study Bible, Romans 8:30.

19. Quest Study Bible, 1 Timothy 2:3.

20. Quest Study Bible, 1 Corinthians 7:23.

21. Quest Study Bible, 1 Corinthians 15:22, 1 Peter 3:18.

22. Quest Study Bible, 1 John 4:11.

23. Quest Study Bible, Psalm 27:10, 1 Peter 5:7.

24. Quest Study Bible, 2 Corinthians 5:27.

25. David Ramsey, *Total Money Makeover*, 2013, (Nelson Books) Nashville, TN, 23-54.

26. Quest Study Bible, Acts 3:25.

27. Quest Study Bible, Hebrews 11:11.

28. Quest Study Bible, Ephesians 2:19.

29. Quest Study Bible, 1 Peter 1:15-16, Romans 11:16.

30. Quest Study Bible, Ephesians 4:30.

31.   Quest Study Bible, Proverbs 1:33, Isaiah 22:23, Proverbs 10:9.

32.   Quest Study Bible, Genesis 11:6-9.

33.   T. Harv Eker, *Secrets of the Millionaire Mind*, Copyright @ 2005 by Harv Eker, New York, NY 18-22.

34.   Mindset Habits, How Does the Mind Work? http://www.mindset-habits.com Mindset Habit, May 20, 2010.

35.   http://www.mindset-habits.com.

36.   Dr. Mary Segars' personal quote, 2010.

37.   Attended Millionaire Mind Experience Seminar, Ramada Inn, Southfield, Michigan, February 2016.

38.   If you talk to yourself, you are a genius, Elite Daily, http://elitedaily.com, July 9, 2015.

39.   Quarterly Journal of Experimental Psychology, Gary Lupvan, Daniel Singley, December 10, 2011.

40.   Shad Helmsteter, PhD., *What to say to yourself when you talk to yourself*, Copyright 1982 by Shad Helmsteter, 7-20.

APPENDIX B

My Pledge

I, _____, have given myself permission to talk to myself as a way of acknowledging my strengths and to encourage myself to be the best me God created. I will only say true things about myself that will encourage me to highlight my strengths and my best attributes, that will increase and make me even better. I am confident in my God-given talents, such as _____ and _____.

If I need to improve in any area of my life, I will be willing to learn new things which will allow me to grow and become a mature person.

I will be kind to me, and in turn, I will be kind to others. I will take care of myself by allowing my body to rest, eating properly, and maintaining a positive attitude about life. If I am not satisfied with things going on in my life, I have the power to change things in my life.

_____

Name   Date

(Note: This is just a sample I used. Please feel free to modify, add, and change to your liking and wording. After all, it is you talking to you!)

APPENDIX C

A List of Negative Words, Phrases to Remove from Your Life

No	Not	Unhappy
Can't	Pessimistic	Unjust
Won't	Poor	Unhealthy
Don't	Quit	Unfair
Afraid	Quitter	Upset
Scared	Reject	Unwanted
Dreadful	Lazy	Unwelcomed
Distress	Sad	Vile
Awful	Sorry	Vindictive
Jealous	Idiot	Weary
Lose	Stupid	Unwise
Loser	Ugly	Worthless
Never		Zero

Feel free to add additional words you want to eliminate from your thoughts, from your speaking, and from your life.

A List of Words to Use, Think, and Speak

I recommend you develop words and phrases to incorporate into your vocabulary to strengthen your self-talk to be more positive and geared toward the words in the Bible.

_____   _____

_____   _____

_____   _____

_____   _____

_____   _____

_____   _____

_____   _____

_____   _____

_____   _____

_____   _____

_____   _____

_____   _____

_____   _____

_____   _____

_____   _____

_____   _____

_____   _____

_____   _____

_____   _____

_____   _____

_____   _____

_____   _____

APPENDIX D

List of Poor Self-Image Characteristics

1. Pessimistic outlook on life.

2. Lack of confidence in social skills.

3. Extreme consciousness about appearance, performance, or status.

4. Fear of being alone.

5. Defensiveness in behavior and conversations.

6. Inability to accept praise.

7. A critical and judgmental view of others.

8. Use of anger as a defense to keep from getting hurt.

9. Inability to express emotions.

10. A tendency to develop clinging relationships.

11. Fear of intimacy, because it might lead to rejection or a smothering relationship.

12. Self-defeating habits and behavior.

13. Self-consciousness about appearance, performance or status.

14. A view of other people as competition to beat, not friends to enjoy.

15. A sense of masculinity or femininity felt only through sexual conquests.

16. A striving to become something or somebody instead of relaxing and enjoying who they are.

APPENDIX E

Campaign Sign

APPENDIX F

Favorite Quotes — Sahaj Kohli

Always believe in the impossible.

~~~~~~~~~~~~~~~~~~~~

Every accomplishment starts with the decision to try.

~~~~~~~~~~~~~~~~~~~~

Love yourself as much as you want to be loved.

~~~~~~~~~~~~~~~~~~~~

Five Things to Tell Yourself Daily:

1. Today will be my day.
2. I'm the best me there is.
3. I know that I am a winner.
4. I can do it; I know I can.
5. God will always be with me.

~~~~~~~~~~~~~~~~~~~~

Be positive and believe in yourself.

~~~~~~~~~~~~~~~~~~~~

Positive Mind. Positive Vibes. Positive Life.

~~~~~~~~~~~~~~~~~~~

Believe you can and you will.

~~~~~~~~~~~~~~~~~~~

Be You!

~~~~~~~~~~~~~~~~~~~

Whatever you believe about yourself on the inside

is what you will manifest on the outside.

~~~~~~~~~~~~~~~~~~~

The fact that someone else loves you

doesn't rescue you from the project of loving yourself.

Favorite Quotes — Coco Chanel

Be at peace with yourself.

~~~~~~~~~~~~~~~~~~~~~

Your mind will always believe everything you tell it.

~~~~~~~~~~~~~~~~~~~~~

Feed it faith. Feed it truth. Feed it with love.

~~~~~~~~~~~~~~~~~~~~~

Beauty begins the moment you decide to be yourself.

Favorite Quotes — Jenna Kutcher

Talk about your blessings more than you talk about your burdens.

~~~~~~~~~~~~~~~~~~~~

Being yourself is the prettiest thing you can be!

~~~~~~~~~~~~~~~~~~~~

Think abundantly. Energy follows intention.

~~~~~~~~~~~~~~~~~~~~

What consumes your mind, controls your life.

~~~~~~~~~~~~~~~~~~~~

Your vibe attracts your tribe.

Favorite Quotes — Other

Speak with Honesty

Think with Sincerity

Act with Integrity

~~~~~~~~~~~~~~~~~~~

What you tell yourself

Every day will either

Lift you up or

Tear you down

~~~~~~~~~~~~~~~~~~~

Don't shush your inner voice.

It's who you really are.

~~~~~~~~~~~~~

Fear happens when we leave our minds empty.

~~~~~~~~~~~~

Believe you can and you're halfway there!

~~~~~~~~~~~~

Don't ever let negative and toxic people

rent space in your head.

Raise the rent and kick them out!

~~~~~~~~~~~~~~~~~~

Believe in Yourself!

~~~~~~~~~~~~~~~~~~

Your mind is a powerful thing.

When you fill it with positive thoughts,

your life will start to change.

~~~~~~~~~~~~~~~~~~~~

Your mind is a garden.

Your thoughts are the seeds.

You can grow flowers or you can grow weeds.

~~~~~~~~~~~~~~

InspirationalQuotesGazette.com:

Stay away from negative people.

They have a problem for every solution.

Made in the USA
Columbia, SC
01 April 2018